A VISION OF IRANSHAHR

Constitution for Change

Latif Simorghi

CONTENTS

To the peoples of Iranshahr,
This age of chaos will pass. The future belongs to you.

The Guarded Domains of Iranshahr

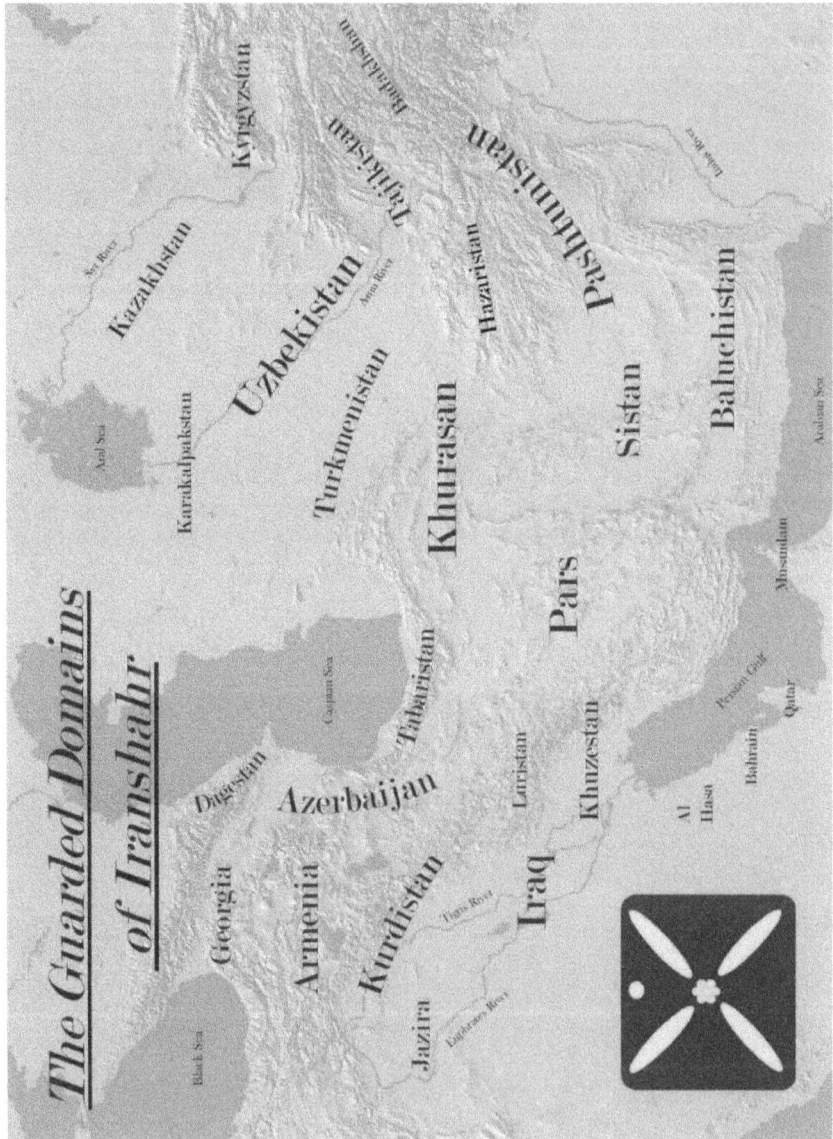

Author's Note

I am humbled and grateful that you wish to take time out of your life to read this small book. These are the simple thoughts of a common person who wishes to see a land close to his heart rise from centuries of a dark age. Most ideas within this book I believe work specifically for Iranshahr, but I am sure that many concepts could be of interest for anyone who is disillusioned with their government, whether a dictatorship, oligarchy, or representative democracy. Before continuing onto the introduction, I must say something important.

I am but a person endowed with all the limitations and strengths of any other human being. My belief system has been created by the genes I have inherited, the culture I was brought up in, the actions of my parents, my interactions with other people, and the random events of my life. I believe I am close to being right, but I know that it is probable that much of my beliefs are still far from the truth.

Do not accept the ideas in this book unconditionally. Be skeptical and compare it with other ideas and systems. Discuss it with friends and foes. Only after reflection and debate should this work be accepted or rejected. Remember that all truths are human truths. Those who claim to know the absolute truth are the most ignorant.

Latif Simorghi

KVIMOTEFINALLATINO

Latif Simorghi

INTRODUCTION

This constitution is for a country that does not exist, at least for the present time. Most people even within Iranshahr do not know this name and assume it is the same as Iran. The two words are related but there are important differences. Iranshahr is the name of geographical location was first mentioned during the Sassanid era (224-651 CE).[1] The extent of this land corresponded with the boundaries of the Sassanid Empire and its vassals; roughly from the Indus River in the East to the Euphrates River in the West, and from the Persian Gulf and Indian Ocean in the South to the Caucasus Mountains and the Caspian and Aral seas in the North.[2] The realm of Iranshahr was divided into seven lands or domains that were vast in their own right but still were just sub regions of this larger entity.[3] The name itself slowly descended into obscurity after the Arab conquests, but the unity of Iranshahr remained a constant feature for most of the last 1,400 years. These natural boundaries and the legacy of Sassanid Shahanshahs (King of kings) as a political ideal created the foundation for a self-contained empire framework.

Whether an Arab caliph, Sistani or Deylami upstart, Turkic slave soldier or chieftain, or Mongol khan, all tried to become "Shahanshah" over the "Empire" (or the Guarded Domains as the last empire in Iranshahr was called under the Qajar dynasty) that comprised Iranshahr.[4] In general, each successive dynasty might have been ethnically different from the one it would replace, but the boundaries of their empires would end roughly at Iranshahr's frontiers. This political continuity was reinforced by the emergence of New Persian as the language of culture among the

---

[1] Touraj Daryaee, *Šahrestānīhā-ī Ērānšahr: a Middle Persian text on late antique geography, epic, and history : with English and Persian translations* (Costa Mesa, Calif.: Mazda Publishers, 2002).

[2] V. V. Bartol' d and Clifford Edmund Bosworth, *An Historical Geography of Iran*, Modern Classics in Near Eastern Studies (Princeton, N.J: Princeton University Press, 1984).

[3] Daryaee, *Šahrestānīhā-ī Ērānšahr*.

[4] A. Shapur Shahbazi, "CROWN Iv. Persian Rulers from Arab Conquerors," in *Encyclopaedia Iranica*, accessed December 5, 2019, http://www.iranicaonline.org/articles/crown-iv.

political elites of Iranshahr, embodied by the literary masterpiece, The *Shahnameh*.[5] At the local level, communities spoke and wrote in their own languages, which interacted with New Persian to create Iranshahr's rich diversity of cultures. The peoples of Iranshahr did not see each other as members of the same nation, but they certainly were not foreigners to one another either. What emerged was a unique geographical entity, a cultural continent like China, India, or Europe, even though this continent lacked a name.

What emerged time and again to govern this vast collection of peoples was a decentralized empire ruled by a Shahanshah. The Shahanshah was the possessor of the "Farr," a concept of legitimacy similar to the Chinese "Mandate of Heaven," or the European "Divine Right of Kings." Farr, or fortune, was given to the king and his or her (mostly his) bloodline as the right to rule.[6] Farr was bestowed from the divine first through the goddess Anahita, symbolized by her giving a golden halo, or through the legendary bird, the Simorgh, symbolized by her shadow or feather passing over the fortunate leader. With the infusion of Islam into Iranshahr, the concept of Farr became connected with the sacredness of the blood of the Prophet.[7] Then with the Turco-Mongol ascendancy, the Farr incorporated the nomadic steppe reverence for the descendants of Chingiz Khan.[8] Fortune, though connected to blood, had to be linked to prestige and the duty to keep chaos from the empire.

The right to rule was not unconditional.[9] Rulers bound by the Shahanshah political framework, had duties and if they failed in those duties, the Farr might pass from them to another within the dynasty or even to new blood. The Shahanshah (or Caliph, Sultan, or Khan) was bound to provide peace and justice to the empire. He had to limit

---

[5] Marshall G. S. Hodgson, *The Classical Age of Islam*, His The Venture of Islam ; v. 1 (Chicago: University of Chicago Press, 1974).

[6] Abolala Soudavar, *The Aura of Kings: Legitimacy and Divine Sanction in Iranian Kingship*, Bibliotheca Iranica, no. 10 (Costa Mesa, Calif: Mazda Publishers, 2003).

[7] Kathryn Babayan, *Mystics, Monarchs, and Messiahs: Cultural Landscapes of Early Modern Iran*, Harvard Middle Eastern Monographs 35 (Cambridge, Mass: Distributed for the Center for Middle Eastern Studies of Harvard University by Harvard University Press, 2002).

[8] Beatrice Forbes Manz, *The Rise and Rule of Tamerlane*, Cambridge Studies in Islamic Civilization (Cambridge ; New York: Cambridge University Press, 1989).

[9] Mehrzad Boroujerdi, ed., *Mirror for the Muslim Prince: Islam and the Theory of Statecraft*, First edition, Modern Intellectual and Political History of the Middle East (Syracuse, New York: Syracuse University Press, 2013).

the political squabbling of the oligarchs who brought him to supreme power, or who's ancestors had brought his ancestors to supreme power. He had to defend the local elites from the oligarchs, and to respect their autonomy to rule the lands they had governed for centuries.[10] The Shahanshah had to guard the trade routes from banditry and tribal raiders for the merchants' profits. He must satisfy the mullahs through "enjoining good and forbidding evil," throughout the empire, mostly by persecuting heretics.[11] He had to protect the peasant, the artisan, or the slave from the tyranny of all those who ruled over them. He had to bolster the prestige of his reign and the name of his dynasty through patronage of the arts and the sciences. And finally, he had to defend the boards of the empire from rival countries. More often than not, this ideal of possessing the Farr was backed purely by raw power, and injustice rather than justice prevailed.

However, if injustice went beyond, what even those brutal times tolerated, then the incompetent or tyrannical Shahanshah was no longer legitimate. A sibling, cousin, uncle, nephew might gain the backing of the oligarchs to overthrow the Shahanshah. A divided oligarchy might create an empire wide civil war to secure their candidate to the throne. The regional elites might decide to govern themselves. The mullahs might raise a mob to attack officials of the corrupt ungodly regime. The peasants might rise up in a wave of desperate revolts. Or from the margins of the empire or society, a tribal chieftain, a messianic religious leader, or the leader of an urban confraternity, might declare the Farr has left the whole decadent system and that they hold the feather of the Simorgh. The losing of Farr was the envelopment of the empire in bloodshed, fragmentation, and foreign invasion. For the Shahanshah to keep the Farr, he had to balance the interests of subjects and limit corruption.

The Shahanshah, through propaganda, tried to portray himself as all powerful, yet his power was limited. The Shahanshah was on paper the "Master of the World" or the "Shadow of God." In actuality he was a first among equals among the oligarchs,

---

[10] Jeffrey A Winters, *Oligarchy* (Cambridge; New York: Cambridge University Press, 2012). The type of oligarchy that the political system in Iranshahr had is called a sultanistic oligarchy. This is where one oligarch stands above the others (a king of kings). This "first among equals" oligarch defends the collective wealth of the oligarchs but keeps the oligarchs in check so that their consolidation of wealth does not lead to popular discontent. The Shahanshahs of old fit very nicely into this idea, but the sultanistic oligarchy is alive and well in Iranshahr. All the dictatorships across the region fall into this type of oligarchy.

[11] Julie Scott Meisami, *The Sea of Precious Virtues* (University of Utah Press, 1991).

and the very fact that his blood was no more special than that of his siblings, cousins, uncles, or nephews meant that he was not indispensable.[12] The geography of Iranshahr is composed of formidable mountain ranges, great deserts, and wide-open steppes.[13] Political centralization was (and still may be) impossible. Armies from the valleys and plains could invade the homes of mountaineers or nomads to enforce a governor or exact tribute but more often than not, those armies had to flee after taking a beating. Wars to bring local elites, tribes, or urban oligarchies directly under the personal rule of the Shahanshah and his ethnic or religious allies were always devastating.[14] Replacing regional elite classes with the new imperial elite associated with the dynasty was also rarely of benefit to the Shahanshah. It was always less costly for everyone involved for the local elites to claim submission to their Shahanshah, but then de facto govern themselves.[15]

In this precarious balance of power, much of the empire was left to local governance, while a limited monarchy managed the larger issues, often with the assistance of the local powers. In a sense, it was almost confederal in nature.[16] There was enough power for the Shahanshah to mobilize for the defense the empire, enough taxes and tribute to sustain his court, and enough homage to maintain his prestige,

---

[12] Winters, *Oligarchy*.

[13] Bartol' d and Bosworth, *An Historical Geography of Iran*.

[14] Kaveh Farrokh, *Iran at War, 1500-1988* (Oxford ; Long Island City, NY: Osprey Publishing, 2011).

[15] Richard W Bulliet, *The Patricians of Nishapur: A Study in Medieval Islamic Social History* (Cambridge: Harvard University Press, 2008).

[16] Parvaneh Pourshariati, *Decline and Fall of the Sasanian Empire: The Sasanian-Parthian Confederacy and the Arab Conquest of Iran* (London ; New York : New York: I.B. Tauris in association with the Iran Heritage Foundation ; Distributed in the U.S.A. by Palgrave Macmillan, 2008). Pourshariati's arguments on the decentralized nature of the Sassanid Empire is very convincing to me. The idea of this empire as a centralized absolute monarch is an attempt to Westernize the Sassanids in my view. The desire to portray the Sassanids in this manner comes from the Western-centric view that centralization is inherently good and modern (the nation-state). Many would like to equate the Iranshahr of the Sassanids to their rivals, the Romans and their neighbors, the Han Empire of China in terms of centralization and the absolute supremacy of the ruler. Iranshahr was definitely less centralized then the two over superpowers of their day, but that does not mean inferior in power or in effectiveness of governing.

but the empire was composed of provinces or satrapies that governed much of the domains. This was the premodern, and conservative, ideal of the Shahanshah system and of Iranshahr, but it worked for a thousand years and endured revolutionary or near cataclysmic events, namely the Islamic transformation, the Golden Age, the Black Death, and several genocidal conquests of the steppe tribes.

The great rupture of this ideal emerged in the 10th century AH (16th century CE), during which politics became ever more entwined with sectarianism. Dominating the heart of Iranshahr were the Sufi-Shia Safavids. Dominating the peripheral, though no less important, lands of Iranshahr were the Legalist-Sunni Ottomans, Shaybanids, and Timurid Mughals. All four were potential successors of the ancient ideal of the Shahanshahs, but each had the strength to repel each other so that frontier zones stabilized and the unity of Iranshahr was thwarted. The division of Iranshahr was part of a slow and painful decline of Muslim dynasties to defend their peoples from foreign aggression.

During this new age of political division in Iranshahr, cultural forces within, and economic forces without, exasperated the decline of all four successor empires of the Shahanshahs. The great flow of trade from China and India to a hungry Europe once enriched Iranshahr. But those days were numbered. The great accident of history, the "discovery" of the Americas, would ensure that Iranshahr's status as the great middleman of Eurasia was no more. The decimation of indigenous peoples throughout the Americas by European arms and Eurasian diseases gave Europeans something they never had before: vast empty spaces of fertile land for resources the rest of the world wanted.[17] Silver and cash crops ripped from American soil through the blood and sweat of African and indigenous slaves flooded through the ports of Europe.[18] That silver would fund an explosion of wars in Europe transforming the art of war into the science of war. That silver would eventually stream into China, but it would not pass through the fingers of Iranshahr's merchants. Instead, with the unstoppable progress of Europe now underway, their ships would sail around Iranshahr, taking their enormous profits with them. Iranshahr would go from the bridge between East and West to an economic backwater.

Just prior to great exploitation of the New World, the innovative and open-minded era of the Islamic Golden age was ending. The ossification of sharia law and the slow triumph of legalist and mystical interpretations of Islam over the rationalist and philosophical strains meant that the rulers of Iranshahr would become more the

---

[17] Jared M. Diamond, *Guns, Germs, and Steel: The Fates of Human Societies* (New York: Norton, 2005).

[18] Eduardo Hughes Galeano, *Open Veins of Latin America (Las Venas Abiertas de América Latina, Engl.). Five Centuries of the Pillage of a Continent* (New York: Monthly Review Press, 1973).

patrons of arts then of the sciences.[19] The unimaginable devastation wrought by the Mongol conquests, the Black Death, and Timur's mass butchery left Iranshahr shattered and inward looking.[20] Order and inner peace were the ideals that emerged in this bleak time, which meant that the borderline heretical musings of philosophers and scientists would no longer be tolerated.[21] With less and less wealth flowing through Iranshahr, even the arts would be sacrificed. By the 1800s, CE, the mullahs would stand triumphant as the sole beneficiaries of weakening regimes.

The empires of Iranshahr would no longer stand under the shadow of the Simorgh, but under the shadow of imperialism. Two foreign powers would dismember Iranshahr piece by piece.[22] The puny successor emirates of the Shaybanids would be conquered by Russia. The Mughals were conquered by Britain and Eastern Khorasan was transformed into the British protectorate of Afghanistan. The Ottoman territories in Iranshahr would remain intact but shaky (the exception being the Caucasus losses to Russia), until the Great War caused the utter collapse of the once mighty empire. Turkey would pry Anatolia back from Britain, Russia, France, and Greece, but it would not be a successor to Iranshahr. Turkish nationalism would abandon the traditions of Iranshahr's multiculturalism and local autonomy for a Westernized unitary nation-state. The Safavids would not see the age of Western Imperialism, for they would collapse earlier, leaving the heart of Iranshahr, called Iran, in a state of civil war for eighty years. The Qajars would rise triumphantly at the top of the old tribal order but would be unprepared for the new world around them. Russia battered the Qajar forces leading to two treaties that still haunt Iranians to this day: Gulistan and Turkmanchey. The Qajars would also be humiliated by the British when the jewel of Khorasan, the city of Herat, would be forged into the British protectorate of Afghanistan rather than be regained by the Qajars. To their credit, the Shahs of Iran did try to play the British and Russians against one another and they were successful in keeping Iran from being

---

[19] S. Frederick Starr, *Lost Enlightenment: Central Asia's Golden Age from the Arab Conquest to Tamerlane* (Princeton University Press, 2015), https://press.princeton.edu/books/paperback/9780691165851/lost-enlightenment.

[20] Marshall G. S. Hodgson, *The Expansion of Islam in the Middle Periods*, His The Venture of Islam ; v. 2 (Chicago: University of Chicago Press, 1974). Hodgson has an amazing chapter looking at the origins of conservativism as a phenomenon within a society.

[21] Timur Kuran, *The Long Divergence: How Islamic Law Held Back the Middle East* (Princeton; Oxford: Princeton University Press, 2013).

[22] Peter Hopkirk, *The Great Game: The Struggle for Empire in Central Asia* (New York: Kodansha International, 1992).

completely conquered.[23] But, their attempt to modernize was impeded by the conservative mullahs and the dynasty's own corruption. The Guarded Domains of Iran could no longer be protected against foreign exploitation. Iranshahr was subjugated to the will of outsiders from then on.

Either due to foreign "divide and conquer" policies or in response to colonial aggression, nationalism took root in Iranshahr. The bonds that held Iranshahr together politically and then culturally would be cut, cord by cord. Russification and the British policy of de-Persianization would co-opt the local elites from their trans-regional Persian language. The foreign powers would promote differences between the peoples such as Azeris and Armenians, Uzbeks and Tajiks, Pashtuns and Hazaras so that their anger would be targeted towards one another instead of their masters. But the independent states of Iranshahr would also destroy their ancient bonds.

Turkey and Pahlavi Iran would raise Turkish and Persian nationalism to new heights. Their one state, one people ideology would lead these governments to carry out ethnic cleansing and cultural genocide of peoples who were by right their equals as a people of Iranshahr.[24] And pan-Arabism would lead the Semitic peoples of Iranshahr to abandon their cultural home for some dream of a pure Arab superstate. Peoples who had lived in relative harmony now competed for the dubious aid of foreign powers or the iron hug of the puppet dictators that arose after colonialism supposedly disappeared. The 14th century AH (20th century CE) further divided Iranshahr into nation-states, each ruled by an authoritarian regime who supported one ethnicity over the others, further integrating nationalism into the bones of Iranshahr. But other "isms" have worked with nationalism to strangle Iranshahr and its peoples.[25]

Now, in our 15th century AH (21st century CE), Iranshahr is in a dreary state, oppressed by ideologies of domination and hate. We have the revival of intense sectarianism and plain religious extremism to compound the woes of Iranshahr. We have neoliberalism and materialism narrowing our minds' aspirations towards profits

---

[23] Roxane Farmanfarmaian, *War and Peace in Qajar Persia: Implications Past and Present*, History and Society in the Islamic World (New York: Routledge, 2015).

[24] Alireza Asgharzadeh, *Iran and the Challenge of Diversity: Islamic Fundamentalism, Aryanist Racism, and Democratic Struggles*, 1st ed (New York: Palgrave Macmillan, 2007).

[25] The "isms" that ravage Iranshahr and much of the world are: nationalism, authoritarianism, neoliberalism, materialism, religious extremism, and sexism.

to the destruction of all else that makes us human.[26] Nationalism has unleashed racism on a horrific scale. And sexism holds our societies back by viewing women as less than human, and incentivizing men to become violent monsters.[27] This cultural continent is a shadow of its old self. It is a chaotic menagerie of weak nation-states, each with an ethnic majority falsely believing in its exceptionalism and its right to oppress the ethnic minorities within those boundaries. Nations extol myths about past glories while languishing in a uninspiring present and a dismal future. These societies of domination entwine the "isms" a culture of oppression which encourages citizens to harm one another to feel a sense of control over their lives.[28]

But what is to be done?

The most common nationalistic responses are secession for minority groups and ethnic cleansing for majority groups. There is little need to speak about ethnic cleansing since it is a damnable action. When a nation-state persecutes minorities into forcing them to flee, wipes out a minority's culture, or slaughters minorities wholesale, those are forms of ethnic cleansing and should not be acceptable within Iranshahr.

Secession is a more complex response and sometimes is the only solution. Within Iranshahr, most minorities face some form of discrimination, and in many cases, face systematic persecution. Pushed into action by their systematic dehumanization by the majority, many ethnic minorities turn to separatist nationalism. Secession has always been a strenuous and dangerous prospect, so only desperate people are drawn to it. If a minority group cannot keep its language, its culture, have political autonomy, or have genuine participation in the country's government then secession is a people's right.

However, it is in the interest of all peoples to stay as one country rather than split into smaller countries for many reasons. The larger the country and the larger the country's population typically means the larger the common market. A dozen little countries have to negotiate with each other to lower tariffs between each other, where, they could trade freely as one united country. Unity also means greater potential for

---

[26] Tim Kasser, *The High Price of Materialism* (Cambridge, Mass: MIT Press, 2002); Wendy Brown, *Undoing the Demos: Neoliberalism's Stealth Revolution* (New York: Zone Books, 2017).

[27] bell hooks, *The Will to Change: Men, Masculinity, and Love*, 1st Atria Books hardcover ed (New York: Atria Books, 2004); Colette Harris, *Control and Subversion: Gender Relations in Tajikistan* (London: Pluto Press, 2004).

[28] Paulo Freire, Donaldo P. Macedo, and Ira Shor, *Pedagogy of the Oppressed*, trans. Myra Bergman Ramos, 50th anniversary edition (New York: Bloomsbury Academic, 2018).

the collective power to defend that country's sovereignty against foreign powers. A dozen little countries are easy pickings for foreign domination versus one large country. Small countries usually require a patron state guarding them against other states. Larger states can hold their own in the international arena. Finally, because of the limited space, the potential for conflict and competition goes up between many tiny independent states versus many states united under a common purpose. These three reasons are demonstrated throughout Iranshahr's history. When Iranshahr was united, there was stability for commerce and innovation. There was enough concentration of power to keep other empires from attacking too often. And more often than not, there was relative peace. If ethnic groups can cooperate in creating a government that protects them as a whole and protects them from each other, then there is no logical reason for secession. This treatise is about a political system that emulates this aspiration and defends the peoples of Iranshahr against the "isms" of which I have spoken.

What I hope to do with this book is to present a possible solution to the woes of Iranshahr. The Commonwealth Constitution is based loosely on the ancient Iranshahr ideal of the Shahanshahs, which I apply to a modern context as the "Guarded Domains Model." The Shahanshah was a king *of* kings, a first prince among other princes, which meant that the empires of Iranshahr were not centralized absolutist states as the European monarchies went, but decentralized states in which regions had considerable autonomy.[29] The European absolutism led to the idea of the nation-state as the central government owning all the power. Iranshahr was ensnared by the nation-state model, so it strayed from the political structure that kept it sovereign. Autonomy and relative tolerance for differences were strengths of the empires of Iranshahr, not weaknesses.[30]

Before I continue with the Guarded Domains model, I need to dispel the reader that I have some romanticized understanding of Iranshahr's past. The past is ruthless, regardless of the region or country. Iranshahr is no different. The Shahanshahs were more likely to be tyrants than guardians of the common person. The noble elites, the merchants, the mullahs were power hungry and exploited the poor masses of peasants or urban mobs. The common person was also crude, willing to kill members of their communities who had ideas that diverged with traditions. Even before the British, the Russians, and the Americans arrived, Iranshahr was not a paradise. It is also true that Western powers brought with them innovations that have transformed Iranshahr and

---

[29] Pourshariati, *Decline and Fall of the Sasanian Empire.*

[30] Amy Chua, *Day of Empire: How Hyperpowers Rise to Global Dominance and Why They Fall* (New York, N.Y.: Anchor Books, 2009). The empire of the Achaemenid Persians is the first of Chua's hyperpowers.

the world for the better. A nationalist blames *only* outside powers for their country's woes. A patriot recognizes the weakness within their country, the cultural flaws that hold a society back. The peoples of Iranshahr must look in the mirror and accept that their cultures' sexism, classism, sectarianism, and corruption strangled Iranshahr long before the foreign powers arrived. Foreign powers exploit weaknesses within a society to divide and conquer. Iranshahr's woes are the result of its ancestors' failings, as well as foreign manipulation.

So to be clear, I do not believe Iranshahr should return to the political structures of the Shahanshahs. We live in the modern era where the people should govern. The age of kings should end in this century. One man rulership has been disastrous for humanity, and we should banish that form of government to the annals of history. What I am interested in, is the idea of a decentralized country composed of multiple ethnic groups that cooperate in maintaining their sovereignty against foreign powers and the ideologies of hatred and division. Modern democracy should be built upon the ability to harness the collective power of multiple peoples in defense of the ancient empire's sovereignty, while allowing those peoples to govern themselves at the local level.

So, what is the Guarded Domains Model? It is a political system that combines aspects of federalism and confederalism to allow different ethnic groups and regions to govern themselves at the local level and govern together at the state level. A federation is a collection of semiautonomous provinces that share power with a central government.[31] A confederation is a collection of sovereign states that band together for a common purpose.[32] At the top of the political structure are the People (the collection of peoples that make up the country) and the embodiment of their will, the

---

[31] Alexander Hamilton et al., eds., *The Federalist Papers*, Civic Classics 3 (New York: Penguin Books, 2012); P.-J. Proudhon and Richard Vernon, *The Principle of Federation* (Toronto; Buffalo: University of Toronto Press, 1979).

[32] Murray Greensmith Forsyth, *Unions of States: The Theory and Practice of Confederation* (New York: Leicester University Press : Holmes & Meier, 1981); Frederick K. Lister, *The Early Security Confederations: From the Ancient Greeks to the United Colonies of New England*, Contributions in Political Science, Global Perspectives in History and Politics, no. 388 (Westport, Conn: Greenwood Press, 1999). Many past confederations formed out of collective defense against a major foreign threat or through economic collaboration to compete. Both of these concerns are at work in Iranshahr so confederation would be of great benefit to the region.

Commonwealth Constitution.[33] Through this constitution, the People establish their rights, limitations, and duties and create the Commonwealth: the central government, similar to a federal government. The Commonwealth is the Shahanshah reborn into a modern democratic government. The Commonwealth defends the Guarded Domains against foreign aggressors, but also establishes trade, taxes the provincial governments, maintains the economy and diplomatic relations, creates laws for problems that affect the whole country like healthcare or climate change, and protects the rights of the People against itself and the regional governments called Satrapies.

A Satrapy is a provincial government with considerable autonomy guaranteed by the Commonwealth Constitution. In order for a province to have Satrapy status, it must have a minimum population size of 50,000 people. For every 50,000 people, the Satrapy gets to send one representative to a branch of the Commonwealth legislature.[34] Satrapial governments can be quite variable, so long as the People of that Satrapy retain the power to transform their governments when their structures no longer work and such political systems do not contradict the Commonwealth Constitution. That means a Satrapial government can be a direct democracy, a constitutional monarchy, an anarchic or communistic state, or any manner of democratic republic.[35] Every Satrapy must have its own constitution, and that document cannot contradict the Commonwealth Constitution. A Satrapy creates laws,

---

[33] Jean-Jacques Rousseau, *The Social Contract*, Penguin Books Great Ideas (New York: Penguin Books, 2006).

[34] Mark Thornton and Marc Ulrich, "Constituency Size and Government Spending," *Public Finance Review* 27, no. 6 (November 1, 1999): 588–98, https://doi.org/10.1177/109114219902700602; Benjamin Bingle, "A Matter of Size: Examining Representation and Responsiveness in State Legislatures and City Councils" (Ph.D., United States -- Illinois, Northern Illinois University, 2016), http://search.proquest.com/docview/1795559337/abstract/37C57A51 C9BA42EDPQ/1; Mathias Wessel Tromborg and Leslie A. Schwindt-Bayer, "Constituent Demand and District-Focused Legislative Representation," *Legislative Studies Quarterly* 44, no. 1 (2019): 35–64, https://doi.org/10.1111/lsq.12217.

[35] Abdullah Öcalan, *Democratic Confederalism*, 2014; "Charter of the Social Contract in Rojava (Syria)," *Koerdisch Instituut Brussel* (blog), February 7, 2014, https://www.kurdishinstitute.be/en/charter-of-the-social-contract/. The Kurds of Turkey and Syria have been showing the promise of decentralized democratic governance founded in anarchist principles.

administers justice, collects taxes from its citizens, and delegates powers to its districts called Shahrestans.

The Shahrestans are semiautonomous districts within Satrapies. They are meant to represent the small or large communities that all together make up the Satrapy. In the spirit of decentralization, the Shahrestan represents the local condition and has the power to check the Satrapy and the Commonwealth when the Shahrestan's local interests are threatened. These districts have power over the land. The extraction of minerals and other land-based resources is decided by the majority of people within a Shahrestan. Higher governments cannot force the people of a Shahrestan to exploit resources. But should the people of a Shahrestan decide to exploit their mineral wealth, a third of the profits goes to the Shahrestan, a third goes to the Satrapy, and a third goes to the Commonwealth. A Shahrestan's autonomy in governance depends on the Satrapial constitution it is under.

Because of the vast diversity of Iranshahr, with countless types of ethnic or religious groups, it is important to allow small communities the option for autonomy. For communities that are smaller than 50,000 people which do not want to be part of a Satrapy for fear that their culture or faith might be marginalized by merging with larger groups, there is the option to become an Enclave.[36] An Enclave is almost identical in the powers it has compared to a Satrapy, but because an Enclave does not meet the minimum population size of 50,000 individuals, it would not have similar representation in the Commonwealth legislature. An Enclave can send a representative to the Commonwealth legislature, however, that representative would not have voting powers but could still speak and lobby for their Enclave's interests. The reason for this inequality of powers is to discourage the proliferation of small, inefficient Enclaves. If Enclaves were given minimum representation, then their votes would be disproportionately influential compared to very large Satrapies. It is also meant to encourage cooperation between communities in forming larger, political units like the Satrapy. If an Enclave grew over time to a population over 50,000 individuals, it would then be upgraded to a Satrapy and receive the appropriate representation at the Commonwealth level.

So far, I have described a federal system of government. The People both elect officials for their Satrapies and for the Commonwealth. There tends to be a hierarchy of power but each government level gets different rights and duties clearly designated

---

[36] Peter H. Wilson, *The Holy Roman Empire: A Thousand Years of Europe's History* (London: Allen Lane, 2016). The idea of enclaves came from my study of the unique political organization of the Holy Roman Empire. It was a vast collection of kingdoms, duchies, free city-states, and tiny bishoprics, all with considerable autonomy and variations in the size of their territories.

by a constitution. The Commonwealth Constitution is meant to be a progressive document to protect the disadvantaged and move societies towards equality. I have written it as a means to combat the "isms" I mentioned above and the other great evil in our world: corruption.[37] However, no matter how logical or beneficial an idea or policy is for people, if they do not believe its good for them, the venture will fail. There are those who look to the future and those who look to the past. For the Peoples of Iranshahr who want equality in all its forms - justice, prosperity, democracy - the Commonwealth Constitution is the document to move them in that direction. For communities who are not ready to let go of certain traditions or hierarchies, or desire to be governed by religious law, then there is a compromise that allows these communities to be part of the Guarded Domains but retain full autonomy.

Here is where the Guarded Domains Model introduces confederalism into the political system. For groups that do not wish to be constricted by the Commonwealth Constitution, to govern themselves in undemocratic ways, then these regions may become Vassal States of the Guarded Domains. Vassal States are completely autonomous regions that can create any form of government they wish. They are officially part of the Guarded Domains, but are governed by their own laws.[38] Vassal States are formed by treaty between itself and the Commonwealth.[39] Their minimum obligation to the Guarded Domains is to pay tribute to the Commonwealth (the same tax rate that Satrapies and Enclaves must pay) for the military protection it provides. All other obligations must be negotiated in the treaty. The Vassal States and the Commonwealth form a confederacy which compels them to work on large issues by consensus.

The final aspect of the Guarded Domains Model I wish to stress before closing is the idea of expansion and secession. Empires have been historically built by conquest and bloodshed. I said this was an empire for the modern era. Therefore, the Guarded Domains of Iranshahr cannot be built on blood but on the desire for peoples and regions to band together voluntarily for protection against a chaotic world. Territories

---

[37] Raymond Fisman and Miriam A. Golden, *Corruption: What Everyone Needs to Know*, What Everyone Needs to Know (New York: Oxford University Press, 2017).

[38] Robert I Frost, *The Oxford History of Poland-Lithuania: Volume 1: The Making of the Polish-Lithuanian Union, 1385-1569*, 2018. Though Iranshahr's history is full of Empires with vassal subjects, the idea of Vassal States for this constitution crystallized after studying the Polish-Lithuanian Commonwealth in which two kingdoms united under one elected monarch, but had separate laws and political cultures.

[39] Forsyth, *Unions of States*.

outside the Guarded Domains cannot be annexed unless the population votes freely and fairly to join it as a Satrapy or Enclave, or if the de facto elites of a region decide to join the Guarded Domains as a Vassal State. Empires have also ended in blood as regions tear themselves away. Again, the Guarded Domains Model is meant for the modern age. Secession is a right for all the political units of the Guarded Domains. A Shahrestan can secede from a Satrapy to join another Satrapy or become an Enclave. A Satrapy or Enclave can secede to become Vassal States. Satrapies, Enclaves, or Vassal States can secede from the Guarded Domains to become independent countries. As this Guarded Domains should be built without blood and expand without blood, then it should be able to shrink or disappear without blood.

This introduction is not meant to be a complete description of the constitution you are about to read, but merely to help you think outside of the nation-state paradigm. Whether or not the Guarded Domains Model is pure fantasy or a legitimate challenger of the nation-state model remains to be seen. It is clear that something must change, if the peoples of Iranshahr are to meet their full potential and find the peace and prosperity that has been lacking for at least two hundred years. My hope is that you will find this constitution at least thought-provoking if not convincing.

This project started after reading through different modern and ancient constitutions.[40] The constitution that struck me most as relevant for Iranshahr was the Swiss Confederation Constitution.[41] The Swiss are famous for their direct democracy, decentralization, and history of sectarian conflict and of compromise.[42] I began writing this document using the Swiss constitution as a template. Over the years, I modified language and the document's structure. I added ideas not found in the Swiss document and removed ideas I felt were not relevant for Iranshahr's situation. Some language was too perfectly written for major changes so I apologize

---

[40] United States and Sam Fink, eds., *The Constitution of the United States of America: To Honor the Two-Hundredth Anniversary, September 17, 1987*, 1st ed (New York: Random House, 1985).

[41] Switzerland, *Federal Constitution of the Swiss Confederation of 18 April 1999: (Status as of 27 September 2009).*, 2009.

[42] Jonathan Steinberg, *Why Switzerland?* (Cambridge: Cambridge Univ. Press, 1996); Clive H. Church and Randolph Conrad Head, *A Concise History of Switzerland*, Cambridge Concise Histories (Cambridge: Cambridge University Press, 2013). Though looking to Switzerland as a model for Iranshahr should be done very skeptically, there are many similarities. Switzerland has rough terrain that prevented centralization. It has linguistic and religious differences but has an overarching culture. It has a history of sectarian strife and foreign intervention.

to the Swiss people for this borrowing. I admire Switzerland and its people's culture and political vitality, so I hope my theft will not offend the Swiss People. I encourage you to find the Swiss Constitution and read it as well to compare with this book.

The Commonwealth Constitution is broken down into titles, which in turn are composed of chapters and sections. Title one is the General Provisions that lays out the aspirations of the Guarded Domains of Iranshahr. Title two sets up the relationship of the Commonwealth to the other political units that make up the Guarded Domains. Title three lays out the actual structure of the Commonwealth government. Title four covers topics that affect building a just society, an engaged citizenry, secession, and more. Title five, speaks of the rights, limitations, and duties given to different groups of people that make up the People. Without further explanation, I give you *The Commonwealth Constitution of the Guarded Domains of Iranshahr.*

THE COMMONWEALTH CONSTITUTION OF THE GUARDED DOMAINS OF IRANSHAHR

Preamble

In the names of our children!
We, the People of Iranshahr,
Desiring justice and freedom,
Sought out the Simorgh in kings, dictators, and clerics
following the hoopoe called time and knowledge.
We have reached the court of the Simorgh,
and looked into the mirror to find that we,
the People of Iranshahr are the Simorgh.[43]
Henceforth, the People shall rule democratically,
protect the ideals of this constitution,
and remain vigilant of tyranny in all its forms.
Through this constitution, and through the discipline
of the People,
Iranshahr shall be the home of the Simorgh once
more.

---

[43] Farīd al-Dīn ' Aṭ ṭ ār, Dick Davis, and Afkham Darbandi, *The Conference of the Birds*, The Penguin Classics (Harmondsworth, Middlesex, England ; New York, N.Y., U.S.A: Penguin Books, 1984). Attar's poem has an underlying political message that is revolutionary even if that was not his intent. The birds believe they need a king to rule over them. After a long journey of trials and tribulations, the remaining birds come to the palace of the Simorgh and look into the pool or mirror to find that they are their king.

TITLE 1 GENERAL PROVISIONS

Article 1 Constitutional Reform

(1) All constitutions of the Guarded Domains of Iranshahr are the embodiment of the People's Will.

(2) Any changes to a constitution must be approved by the citizens which that constitution serves.

(3) Because much conflict in the world is due to interpretation of documents, constitutions shall be interpreted literally.

Article 2 Land of Iranshahr

(1) Iranshahr is a region of the world that is rich in diversity, yet interconnected through a common history and culture. The land of Iranshahr stretches from the Indus River, the Pamir Mountains, and the Syr Darya to the Euphrates and the edges of the Zagros. Iranshahr starts at the Persian Gulf and ends at the Caucasus and the Aral Sea.

(2) The Guarded Domains of Iranshahr shall not claim these lands but any territory that wishes to join the Guarded Domains in confederacy or union may do so.

Article 3 Guarded Domains of Iranshahr

(1)The People and the Satrapies of Kurdistan, Iraq, Dagestan, Armenia, Azerbaijan, Talyshstan, Gilan, Mazanderan, Golestan, Luristan, Khuzestan, Pars, Khorasan, Sistan, Baluchistan, Turkmenistan, Hazarastan, the Aimak Republic, Nuristan, Pashtunistan, Karakalpakstan, Uzbekistan, Tajikistan, Badakhshan, the Qashqai Republic, the Bakhtiari Republic, Bahrain, Qatar, al-Hasa Republic, and any region that voluntarily joins the Guarded Domains, form the Guarded Domains of Iranshahr.[44]

---

[44] This list of "Satrapies" is just to show what Iranshahr could look like if all the major ethnic groups united for one common purpose. Satrapies would not necessarily need to be formed along ethnic lines, but could be regional (Satrapy of Transoxiana).

(2) The People of Iranshahr reject the nation-state model due to its exclusive nature and due to the nature of Iranshahr, which favors diversity and tolerance, and has no majority ethnic group.

Article 4 Purpose of Political System
(1) The Guarded Domains of Iranshahr, through the Commonwealth Government and the Satrapies, protects the liberty and sovereignty of the People.
(2) It safeguards the sovereignty and security of the country.
(3) It promotes common welfare, sustainable development, civic virtue, assabiyah, and cultural diversity of the country.[45]
(4) It ensures equal opportunities for all individuals.
(5) It protects the long-term preservation of natural resources and creates policies to lessen the effects of climate change.
(6) It strives to create amiable relations with neighboring countries and promote a peaceful and just international order.
(7) It strives to reduce the influence of nationalism, sexism, racism, classism, materialism, neoliberalism, sectarianism, authoritarianism, and corruption within the societies of Iranshahr.

Article 5 Satrapies
The Satrapies are sovereign insofar as their sovereignty is not limited by the Commonwealth Constitution; they exercise all rights not transferred to the Commonwealth.

Article 6 Language
There shall be no National Language. The Languages of Administration of the Commonwealth government shall be Persian, Arabic, and Turkish. Each Satrapy shall decide its own Language of Administration. All official Commonwealth documents shall be translated into every Satrapial Language of Administration.

---

[45] Richard Dagger, *Civic Virtues: Rights, Citizenship, and Republican Liberalism*, Oxford Political Theory (New York: Oxford University Press, 1997); Ibn Khaldūn and Franz Rosenthal, *The Muqaddimah: An Introduction to History* (Princeton, N.J: Princeton University Press, 1980). Assabiyah is a term coined by Ibn Khaldūn meaning "group solidarity." Uniting the many peoples of Iranshahr with a democratic republican spirit that is anti-nationalist, environmentalist, anti-neoliberal, feminist, anti-materialist, religiously tolerant, and anti-imperialist is the assabiyah to bring Iranshahr out of its dark age into a new era of prosperity and harmony.

Article 7 Rule of Law

(1) The law is the basis for and limitation of government activity.

(2) Government activity must be in the public interest.

(3) Public institutions and private entities shall act in good faith.

(4) No individual or institution is above the law.

Article 8 Individual and Social Responsibility

Every individual is responsible for oneself and advances, according to one's abilities, the goals of state and society.

TITLE 2 COMMONWEALTH, SATRAPIES, AND SHAHRESTANS

CHAPTER 1 RELATIONSHIP BETWEEN THE COMMONWEALTH AND THE SATRAPIES

Section 1 Composition of the Guarded Domains

Article 1 Structure of the Guarded Domains
(1) The Guarded Domains of Iranshahr shall be composed of a federal structure between the central government called the Commonwealth and the semi-autonomous territories called the Satrapies, Nomadic Tribes, and Enclaves.
(2) The Guarded Domains of Iranshahr shall be composed of a confederal structure between the Commonwealth and autonomous territories called Vassal States.

Article 2 Political Units
(1) The founding political structure shall be the Shahrestan.

(2) One or more Shahrestans with a combined population of 50,000 individuals shall compose a Satrapy.

(3) The Satrapies shall unite under the Commonwealth, which shall be the central government of the Guarded Domains of Iranshahr.

(4) Nomadic Tribes may form mobile Satrapies, Shahrestans, or Enclaves. Nomadic groups with a population less than 50,000 individuals may create a mobile Enclave. Nomadic groups with more than 50,000 individuals may form a mobile Satrapy. Mobile Shahrestans and Satrapies shall have the same rights and duties as their fellow Shahrestans and Satrapies.

(5) Vassal States are autonomous territorial units that are not legally bound to the Commonwealth Constitution, but are bound to the Guarded Domains of Iranshahr through negotiations with the Commonwealth.

(6) One or more Shahrestans with a combined population of less than 50,000 individuals shall compose an Enclave.

Article 3 Note on the Status of the Enclave
(1) The Enclave shall enjoy the same rights and duties of the Satrapy written in this constitution excepting the right to representation in the Commonwealth legislature.

(2) Should the population of an Enclave grow to 50,000 individuals or more, its status shall be upgraded to that of a Satrapy.

(3) From this section forward all mentions of Satrapial rights and duties shall be synonymous with Mobile Satrapy and Enclave rights and duties, excepting those mentions relating to the Commonwealth legislature.

Section 2 Tasks of the Commonwealth and the Satrapies

Article 4 Tasks of the Commonwealth
(1) The Commonwealth accomplishes all tasks allocated to it by the Constitution.

(2) The Commonwealth assumes the tasks requiring uniform regulation across the Guarded Domains.

Article 5 Tasks of the Satrapies
The Satrapies accomplish all tasks allocated to them by the Constitution.

Article 6 Tasks of the Shahrestans
The Shahrestans accomplish all tasks allocated to them by the Constitution and the Satrapial constitutions to which they belong.

Section 3 Cooperation between the Commonwealth and the Satrapies

Article 7 Principles

(1) The Commonwealth and Satrapies support each other in the fulfillment of their responsibilities and work together.

(2) The Commonwealth and Satrapies grant each other consideration, support, and administrative and judicial assistance.

(3) Disputes between Satrapies or between Satrapies and the Commonwealth are as far as possible resolved through negotiation or mediation, prior to arbitration.

Article 8 Participation in Commonwealth Decision Making

(1) The Satrapies participate, according to the Constitution, in Commonwealth decision-making, particularly regarding legislation.

(2) The Commonwealth timely and comprehensively informs the Satrapies of its projects; it obtains their consideration whenever their interests are concerned.

Article 9 Implementation of Commonwealth Law

(1) The Satrapies implement Commonwealth legislation according to the Constitution and the law.

(2) The Commonwealth leaves the Satrapies as much organizational scope as possible and takes into account the peculiarities of Satrapies.

(3) The Commonwealth takes into account the financial burden associated with implementing the Commonwealth law by leaving or allocating sufficient financial resources to the Satrapies for the purposes of implementation in an equitable manner.

Article 10 Autonomy of the Satrapies

The Commonwealth preserves the autonomy of the Satrapies.

Article 11 Intersatrapial Treaties

(1) The Satrapies may adopt intersatrapial treaties and create common associations and institutions. They may fulfill tasks of regional interest together without the involvement of the Commonwealth.

(2) The Commonwealth may participate within the limits of its capabilities.

(3) Intersatrapial treaties may not be contrary to the law or interest of the Commonwealth or to the rights of other Satrapies. They have to be made known to the Commonwealth.

Article 12 Supremacy of and Respect for Commonwealth Law

(1) Commonwealth law takes precedence over contrary Satrapial law.

(2) The Commonwealth ensures the adherence to the Commonwealth law by the Satrapies.

Section 4 Shahrestan Powers

Article 13 Autonomy of Shahrestans

(1) The autonomy of the Shahrestans shall be guaranteed within the limits fixed by Satrapial constitution and the Constitution.

(2) In its activity, the Commonwealth takes into account the possible consequences for the Shahrestans.

(3) In particular, it takes into account the special situation of cities, tribes, agglomerations, and mountainous regions.

(4) The Constitution shall allocate exploitation rights of natural wealth to the Shahrestans.

Section 5 Commonwealth Guarantees

Article 14 Satrapial Constitutions

(1) Every Satrapy adopts a democratic constitution. The Satrapial constitution must be approved by the People domiciled in that Satrapy, and must be subject to revision if a majority of the People so require.

(2) The Satrapial constitutions must be guaranteed by the Commonwealth. The Commonwealth grants this guarantee, if the constitutions are not contrary to Commonwealth law.

Article 15 Constitutional Order

(1) The Commonwealth protects the constitutional order of the Satrapies.

(2) It intervenes if the inner order of a Satrapy is disturbed or threatened and cannot be protected by the Satrapy alone or with the help of other Satrapies.

Article 16 Existence and Territory of the Satrapies

(1) The Commonwealth protects the existence and the territory of the Satrapies.

(2) Modifications of the number of the Satrapies are subject to the assent of the population concerned, of the Satrapies concerned, the Shahrestans concerned, and of the People and the Satrapies.

(3) Modifications of the territory of a Satrapy are subject to the assent of the population concerned, the Shahrestans concerned, of the Satrapies concerned.

(4) Intersatrapial boundary settlements may be made by treaty between the Satrapies concerned.

Section 6 Vassal States

Article 17 Relationship to the Guarded Domains

A Vassal State shall establish its relationship to the Commonwealth and to the Guarded Domains as a whole through negotiated treaties between the de facto leadership of the territory seeking vassalage and the Commonwealth; to be agreed upon before incorporation as a political unit of the Guarded Domains.

Article 18 Tribute for Protection

(1) A Vassal State shall pay taxes to the Commonwealth in the manner similar to that of the Satrapies.

(2) In return, the Commonwealth shall extend its military duties to the territory of the Vassal State.

Article 19 Autonomy from the Constitution

(1) A Vassal State shall establish its own government and legislate its own laws without consideration to the Commonwealth Constitution.

(2) Vassal laws must conform to established treaties between itself and the Commonwealth.

Article 20 Subjects of the Guarded Domains

Individuals domiciled in a Vassal State shall not be considered citizens of the Guarded Domains of Iranshahr.

Article 21 Bound to Local Laws

(1) Individuals domiciled in a Vassal State but travelling outside its jurisdiction are subject to the laws of the Guarded Domains of Iranshahr.

(2) Citizens of the Guarded Domains travelling in a Vassal State are subject to the laws of the Vassal State.

Article 22 Integration into the Guarded Domains

(1) A Vassal State may become a Satrapy or Enclave if the following are met:

a. A majority of individuals domiciled in the Vassal State votes for integration during a referendum.

b. The Vassal State in question adopts the Commonwealth Constitution and modifies local laws and processes of governance in accordance with the Constitution.

c. A majority of citizens of the Guarded Domains of Iranshahr vote to accept the Vassal State's integration request in a Commonwealth referendum.

CHAPTER 2 POWERS

Section 1 Relations with Foreign Countries

Article 1 Foreign Relations

(1) Foreign Relations are a Commonwealth matter.

(2) The Commonwealth strives to preserve the independence of the Guarded Domains of Iranshahr and its welfare.

(3) The Commonwealth shall promote cooperative and peaceful relations with countries within the geographical limits of Iranshahr; it shall, in particular, promote the reunification of Iranshahr through negotiation and incentivization.

(4) The Commonwealth shall work to alleviate poverty in the world, to promote respect for human rights, democratic values, and the peaceful coexistence of countries, and to collaborate with other countries to combat climate change and preserve natural resources.

(3) The Commonwealth takes into consideration the powers and interests of the Satrapies when creating foreign policy.

(4) Citizens may propose legislation regarding Foreign Policy.

Article 2 Participation of the Satrapies in Decisions of Foreign Policy

(1) The Commonwealth shall work with the Satrapies in the preparation of foreign policy decisions which concern the Satrapies' essential interests or their powers.

(2) The Commonwealth informs the Satrapies timely and fully and consults them.

(3) The involvement of the Satrapies has particular importance when their powers are concerned. In such cases, the Satrapies participate in international negotiations as partners of the Commonwealth.

Article 3 Relations between the Satrapies and Foreign Countries

(1) Within the scope of their powers, the Satrapies may conclude treaties with foreign countries.

(2) These treaties may not be contrary to the law or to the interests of the Commonwealth or to the laws of other Satrapies. Before concluding a treaty, the Satrapies must inform the Commonwealth.

(3) The Satrapies may deal directly with lower ranking foreign authorities; in other cases, the Commonwealth acts on behalf of the Satrapies.

Section 2 Security, Commonwealth, and Civil Defense

Article 4 Security

(1) The Commonwealth and the Satrapies ensure the security of the country and the protection of the population within the framework of their powers.

(2) They coordinate their efforts in domestic security.

Article 5 Declaration of War

(1) The declaration and directing of war is a Commonwealth matter.

(2) In the event of invasion by enemy forces, the Satrapies may direct Satrapial forces in coordination with the Commonwealth.

Article 6 The Defense Forces

(1) The Guarded Domains of Iranshahr shall have armed forces for the purposes of security and defensive warfare.

(2) The Defense Forces of Iranshahr shall consist of the Savaran, the Commonwealth Militia, the Navy, the Air Force, and the Nonviolent Defense Force. [46]

(3) The Defense Forces contribute to prevent war and to maintain peace; they defend the Guarded Domains's sovereignty and protect the peoples of Iranshahr. They lend support to the Commonwealth and the Satrapial government authorities when they must repel serious threats to domestic security or deal with other exceptional circumstances. The Defense Forces conduct research and development in the fields of military science and technologies to enhance defensive warfare. The statute may provide for further tasks.

(4) The use and maintenance of the Defense Forces is under the authority of the Commonwealth.

(5) The Defense Forces are subordinate to the civilian government of the Commonwealth.

Article 7 Satrapial Guards

(1) The Satrapies have the right to create, operate, and maintain Satrapial guards.

(2) The Satrapies may engage their Guards to maintain public order in their jurisdiction, if the means of the civil authorities no longer suffice to repel serious threats to domestic security.

(3) The Commonwealth may request the use of Satrapial guards in times of war. The Satrapies have the right to refuse such a request.

(4) The number of Satrapial guards per Satrapy is capped at 5,000 troops.

---

[46] Kaveh Farrokh, *The Armies of Ancient Persia: The Sassanians*, 2017. The Savaran were the military elite of Sassanid Iranshahr. This warrior class was the backbone of Sassanid Empire's defense.

Article 8 Peace Guards

(1) The Satrapies shall create peace guards to enforce the laws established by the Satrapies and the Commonwealth.

(2) Peace Guard departments shall have oversight committees composed of civilians living in the communities under these departments' jurisdictions.

Article 9 Militias

(1) Militias shall be maintained and operated by citizens.

(2) The Commonwealth and the Satrapies may not create militias.

(3) In times of war, the Commonwealth may request the service of willing militias. The militias have the right to refuse.

Article 10 Military Service

(1) Military service is voluntary.

(2) The Commonwealth under no circumstances may enact a draft.

(3) Citizens that serve in the Defense Forces and thereby suffer health impairment or die have the right for themselves or their relatives to adequate support by the Commonwealth.

(4) Citizens that serve in the Satrapial Guards and thereby suffer health impairment or die have the right for themselves or their relatives to adequate support by the Satrapy they served.

Article 11 Organization and Preparation of the Defense Forces

(1) Legislation on the military and on the organization, the instruction, and the equipment of the Defense Forces is a Commonwealth matter.

(2) Within the limits of Commonwealth law, the Satrapies have the power to form Satrapial guards, to appoint and to promote officers of such guards, and to furnish a part of their clothing and equipment.

(3) The Commonwealth may take over military installations of the Satrapies against fair compensation.

Article 12 Commonwealth Civil Defense

(1) Legislation on civil defense is a Commonwealth matter.

(2) The Commonwealth Civil Defense protects individuals and property against the results of armed conflicts or natural disasters.

(2) The Commonwealth legislates on the use of civil defense during emergencies.

(3) Civil defense service is voluntary.

(4) The Commonwealth legislates on fair compensation for loss of income.

(5) Individuals who serve in civil defense and thereby suffer health impairment or die have the right for themselves or their relatives to adequate support by the Commonwealth.

Section 3 Education, Research, and Culture

Article 13 Education
(1) Primary education shall consist of nine years and secondary education shall consist of four years.
(1) Primary and secondary education are a Satrapial matter.
(2) The Satrapies ensure a sufficient primary and secondary education open to all children. This education is mandatory and shall be placed under Satrapy direction or supervision. It is free of charge in public schools.
(3) Tertiary education is a Satrapial matter.
(4) The quality of education shall be equivalent for all students domiciled within a Satrapy.
(5) Every student must learn the following subjects by graduation from secondary education:
a. Mathematics including Basic Arithmetic, Geometry, Algebra
b. Basic Physics
c. Basic Chemistry
d. Basic Biology including Evolutionary Theory
e. Basic Ecology
f. Scientific Method
g. World History
h. Iranshahr Geography
i. World Geography
j. Satrapial Language
k. Guarded Domains's Language of Administration
l. International Language
m. Iranshahr Literature
n. World Literature
o. Art
p. Physical Education

Article 14 Language Education
(1) The language in which public school classes are taught shall be determined by the Satrapies.
(2) Primary education must provide students with a proficiency in at least three languages.

(3) The languages shall consist of one local language, the Guarded Domains's language of administration, and one international language.

Article 15 Commonwealth Core Courses

(1) The Commonwealth shall make mandatory the Commonwealth Core Courses for every primary and secondary school.

(2) The Commonwealth Core Courses shall be taught by teachers specially trained to teach these courses.

(3) The Commonwealth is responsible for hiring and paying Commonwealth Core Course teachers.

(4) Every student must learn the following Core Course subjects by graduation from secondary education:

a. Health Literacy including nutrition, sexual education, and mental illness

b. Philosophies and Religions of Iranshahr

c. World Philosophies and Religions

d. Ethnicities of Iranshahr

e. Public Speaking and Debate

f. Political Philosophy

g. History of Iranshahr

h. Critical Thinking

i. Commonwealth Constitution

j. Current Events

k. Life Skills including personal finance, cooking, and cleaning

Section 4 Environment and Zoning

Article 16 Sustainable Development

All levels of government shall strive to use resources efficiently and in a manner that protects natural vitality, social wellbeing, and economic viability.

Article 17 Environmental Policy

(1) The Commonwealth shall legislate on the protection of human health and the natural environment against nuisance and harm caused by human activity.

(2) It ensures that harmful influences are banned and nuisances are avoided. The polluters pay for the costs of avoidance and removal, and may be annually fined until their practices no longer cause harm or nuisance.

(3) Commonwealth regulations shall be implemented by the Satrapies, insofar as the law does not reserve this for the Commonwealth.

(4) The Satrapies may legislate on their own environmental policies so long as they do not conflict with Commonwealth environmental legislation.

Article 18 Zoning

(1) The Commonwealth creates principles on zoning. Zoning falls to the Satrapies and serves to achieve an appropriate, moderate, and sustainable use of the land and its ordered inhabitation.

(2) The Commonwealth encourages and coordinates the efforts of the Satrapies and collaborates with them.

(3) In fulfilling their tasks, the Commonwealth and the Satrapies take the needs of zoning into account.

(4) In particular, zoning shall not favor the encroachment of urban, suburban, or industrial development into rural land.

(5) All agricultural or pastoral lands cannot be rezoned for development. All agricultural and pastoral land shall be protected from development.

Article 19 Water Management

(1) The Commonwealth ensures the sustainable use and the protection of water resources and fights against water mismanagement, within the limits of its powers.

(2) It establishes principles on the sustainable use of water reserves, on the use of water for agricultural and industrial purposes, and on other interventions into the water cycle.

(3) It legislates on drinking water, on securing sufficient residual water, on the safety of dams, on hydraulic engineering, and on interventions to influence precipitation.

(4) The Satrapies dispose of their water resources. Within the limits of Commonwealth law, they may levy dues for water use. The Commonwealth has the right to use waterways for its traffic enterprises; it pays dues and compensation for this use.

(5) On rights concerning international or intersatrapial water resources and dues connected with them, the Commonwealth decides in consultation with the Satrapies concerned. If the Satrapies concerned cannot agree on rights to intersatrapial water reserves, the Commonwealth shall decide.

(6) In fulfilling its tasks, the Commonwealth takes into account the interests of the Satrapies from which the water originates.

Article 20 Coastlines

(1) The Commonwealth ensures that coastlines fulfill their protective, social, and economic functions.

(2) It establishes principles for the protection of coastlines.

(3) All land one hundred meters from an ocean or a sea at high tide shall be considered coastlines and thus public land.

(4) Private land within these hundred meters shall remain private land unless it is sold to the government or a land trust at market value.

(5) Coastlines shall not be developed if they are not already developed.

Article 21 Forests

(1) The Commonwealth ensures that forests fulfill their protective, social, and economic functions.

(2) It establishes principles for the protection of forests.

(3) The Commonwealth encourages measures for the conservation of forests.

(4) Forest land may not be used for development of any kind.

(5) Forest land harvested must be replanted in a manner to maintain forest vitality and diversity.

Article 22 Cultural and Natural Heritage

(1) The protection of cultural and natural heritage is both a Commonwealth and a Satrapial matter.

(2) Together, they establish the principles for the protection of scenery, localities, historical sites, and natural and cultural monuments. In particular, they identify and designate sites for this protected status.

(3) The Satrapies manage designated sites within their territories.

(4) The Commonwealth may by contract or by expropriation, acquire or secure privately owned objects or properties of natural or historical importance. The Commonwealth may transfer management over these objects or properties to the Satrapies. If a Satrapy cannot maintain the integrity of a site, it may transfer management of the site to the Commonwealth.

(5) The Commonwealth legislates on the protection of plant and animal life, and on the preservation of their natural environment and diversity. It protects threatened and endangered species from extinction.

(6) Unique landscapes shall be protected. No installations shall be built on them, and no alterations of any kind may be made to the land. An exception is made for installations serving to ensure their protection or continuation of existing agricultural use.

(7) Buildings with unique architectural traits or historical significance shall be protected. No buildings older than 1950 can be demolished without approval from the relevant Satrapy and Commonwealth.

Article 23 Fishery and Hunting

(1) The Satrapies legislate on the exercise of fishery and hunting, in particular to preserve diversity of fish, game, and birds.

(2) If Satrapial laws endanger the survival of an endangered or threatened species, the Commonwealth may use measures to protect these species.

Article 24 Protection of Animals
(1) The Commonwealth legislates on the protection of animals.
(2) It regulates:
a. the use of animals;
b. the keeping and care of animals;
c. the slaughter of animals;
d. the importation of animals and animal products;
e. trade in animals and transportation of animals;
f. research using live animals;
g. the protection of threatened or endangered animals.
(3) The Commonwealth regulations shall be implemented by the Satrapies, insofar as the statute does not reserve this for the Commonwealth.

Section 5 Public Works and Transportation

Article 25 Public Works
(1) In the interest of the Guarded Domains of Iranshahr or a large part of the country, the Commonwealth may build and operate public works or promote the creation of such works.
(2) The Commonwealth must work with Satrapies affected by such projects.
(3) When public works require the use of private property, directly or indirectly, the Commonwealth must fairly compensate owners before such projects can begin.

Article 26 Commonwealth Granary System
(1) The Commonwealth shall establish and maintain a Commonwealth granary system throughout the Guarded Domains.
(2) The Commonwealth shall ensure that the Guarded Domains has an adequate supply of grain and fodder for a three year period.
(3) The Commonwealth may purchase grains or fodders in times of abundance and sell grains or fodders directly to the public in times of scarcity for prices that are not exploitative.
(4) The Commonwealth shall sell or donate any grain or fodder six months prior to its anticipated spoilage.
(5) The Commonwealth is responsible for the quality and safety of the grains and fodders stored in the Commonwealth granary system.
(6) The Satrapies may establish and maintain their own Satrapial granaries if deemed necessary.

Article 27 Commonwealth Cistern System

(1) The Commonwealth shall establish and maintain a Commonwealth cistern system throughout the empire.

(2) The Commonwealth ensures that the Guarded Domains has an adequate supply of fresh water for a three year period.

(3) The Commonwealth is responsible for the quality and safety of the water stored in the Commonwealth cistern system.

(4) The Satrapies may establish and maintain their own Satrapial cisterns if deemed necessary.

Article 28 Maintenance of the Qanats, Canals, and Dams

(1) The Satrapies shall maintain the qanats, canals, and dams within their borders.

(2) The Commonwealth may assist any Satrapy that cannot fully maintain its qanats, canals, or dams.

Article 29 Bridges

(1) The Commonwealth legislates on standards for bridge construction and safety.

(2) The maintenance of bridges is a Satrapial matter.

(3) The maintenance of bridges may be paid through bridge tolls.

(4) The Commonwealth may assist any Satrapy that cannot fully maintain bridges.

Article 30 Roads

(1) The Commonwealth legislates on standards for road construction and traffic.

(2) The maintenance of roads is a Satrapial matter.

(3) The maintenance of roads may be paid through road tolls.

(4) The Commonwealth may assist any Satrapy that cannot fully maintain its roads.

Article 31 Commonwealth Highways and Satrapial Highways

(1) The Commonwealth ensures the construction and maintenance of a network of Commonwealth highways and the utilization of these highways.

(2) The Satrapies build and maintain their Satrapial highways according to the rules established by the Commonwealth.

(3) The maintenance of highways may be paid through road tolls.

Article 32 Other Transportation

The legislation on navigation, aviation, rail traffic, cable cars, and space travel is a Commonwealth matter.

Article 33 Hiking Trails and Footpaths
Hiking trails and footpaths are a Satrapial matter.

Section 6 Energy and Communication

Article 34 Energy Policy
(1) Within their capabilities, the Commonwealth and the Satrapies strive to create an appropriate, diversified, stable, and economical energy supply compatible with the protection of the environment and human health and the sustainable use of energy.

(2) The Commonwealth establishes principles on the production and use of renewable energy and fossil fuels.

(3) The Commonwealth legislates on the use of energy for installations, vehicles, and appliances. It promotes the research and development of energy techniques that minimize harm to the environment and human health, while increasing efficient and economical use of energy.

(4) The Satrapies legislate on the use of energy in buildings.

(5) The Commonwealth's energy policy takes into account the efforts of the Satrapies and Shahrestans. It takes into account the conditions and economic limitations in the various regions.

(6) The Commonwealth shall work towards energy independence of the Guarded Domains.

Article 35 Renewable Energy
(1) The Commonwealth shall promote renewable energy production and use through legislation, research, and public works.

(2) Satrapial use of renewable energy must increase by a minimum of one percent every year.

(3) Satrapies may request assistance from the Commonwealth if reaching a one percent increase proves difficult.

(4) The Commonwealth strives to shift the Guarded Domains away from the use of fossil fuels to renewable energy sources.

Article 36 Nuclear Energy
(1) Legislation in the field of nuclear energy is a Commonwealth matter.

(2) The Guarded Domains of Iranshahr shall not produce or own nuclear weapons of any kind.

Article 37 Transportation of Energy
(1) The Commonwealth legislates on electricity supply and transportation.

(2) The Commonwealth legislates on pipelines for the transport of liquid or gaseous fuels.

Article 38 Postal and Telecommunication Services

(1) Postal and telecommunication services are a Commonwealth matter.

(2) The Commonwealth ensures sufficient and reasonable postal and telecommunication services in all Satrapies. The rates are fixed according to fair and uniform principles.

Article 39 Radio, Television, and Internet

(1) Legislation on radio, television, internet, and other forms of public telecasting of features and information is a Commonwealth matter.

(2) Providers of radio, television, and the internet content contribute to education, civic engagement, and culture. They contribute to the free formation of opinion, and to the entertainment of the listeners, viewers, and users. They take into account the particularities of the Guarded Domains and the needs of the Satrapies. They present events and information factually, and reflect diverse opinions fairly and adequately.

(3) The independence of radio, television, and the internet and the autonomy of their programming or content development are guaranteed.

(4) It shall be possible to submit complaints about programs or content to an independent authority.

(5) The Commonwealth ensures that internet service providers enable access to all content and applications regardless of the source and without favoring or blocking particular products or websites.

Section 7 Economy

Article 40 Principles of Economic Order

(1) The Commonwealth and the Satrapies protect the principle of economic freedom.

(2) They defend the Commonwealth economy and, together with the private sector of the economy, contribute to the prosperity and economic security of the population.

(3) They create economic policies that favor all classes within society. They do not prioritize the aspirations of the economic elites.

(4) While not harming the interests of the People, they strive to facilitate favorable conditions for the private sector of the economy.

(5) The Commonwealth may deviate from the principle of economic freedom, if such economic freedoms contribute to lower quality of life for the People, environmental degradation, or substantial economic, political, or social inequality in the Guarded Domains.

(6) The Commonwealth prohibits economic activity that exploits individuals or communities.

Article 41 Private Economic Activity

(1) The Commonwealth legislates on the exercise of private economic activity.

(2) It strives to create a unified economic zone in the Guarded Domains. It guarantees that individuals having a university or vocational education or a Commonwealth or Satrapy-recognized education certificate may exercise their profession throughout the Guarded Domains.

Article 42 Competition Policy

(1) The Commonwealth protects against anticompetitive practices in the private sector.

(2) It legislates

a. to prevent price fixing by businesses and organizations.

b. against unfair competition.

c. to prevent two separate businesses from forming a de facto monopoly.

d. to disassemble any business that has a monopoly.

Article 43 Consumer Protection

(1) The Commonwealth legislates on measures to protect consumers against unfair, deceptive, and fraudulent business practices.

(2) It creates principles regarding truthful advertising and product labeling.

Article 44 Banking and Insurance

(1) The Commonwealth legislates on banking and finance; it takes into account the specific task and position of the Satrapial financial institutions.

(2) It legislates on insurance.

Article 45 Monetary Policy

(1) Legislation on money and currency are a Commonwealth matter. The Commonwealth has the right to coin money and to issue bank notes.

(2) The Central Bank of Iranshahr follows a monetary policy which serves the general interest of the Guarded Domains and the People. It shall be an independent central bank, though it is administered with the cooperation and under the supervision of the Commonwealth.

(3) The Central Bank of Iranshahr reserves a sufficient portion of its profits to be used during a recession or depression.

(4) The Central Bank of Iranshahr credits at least two-thirds of its net profits to the Satrapies.

Article 46 Economic Development

(1) The Commonwealth takes measures to ensure sustainable economic development, low unemployment, and low inflation.

(2) It takes into account the economic development of the various regions. It cooperates with the Satrapies and the Shahrestans to ensure development projects correspond with community aspirations and needs.

(3) Regarding credit and currency, foreign trade, and public finance, it may depart from the principle of economic freedom, if deemed necessary.

(4) In their budgetary policies, the Commonwealth, Satrapies, and Shahrestans take into account the sustainable economic development.

(5) In the event of an economic crisis, the Commonwealth may temporarily depart from the principles of economic freedom to stabilize the economy.

Article 47 Foreign Trade

(1) The Commonwealth safeguards the interests of the Commonwealth economy abroad.

(2) In certain cases, it may take measures to protect the Guarded Domains's economy against unfair or unsustainable trade practices of other countries. It may depart from the principle of economic freedom, if deemed necessary.

(3) The Commonwealth has the right to use tariffs if such measures are necessary for a sustainable economy.

Article 48 Supply of Essential Goods and Services

The Commonwealth ensures the Guarded Domains's supply of essential goods and services in case of war, hostile foreign economic restrictions, disasters, or of severe shortages which the economy cannot counteract through market forces. It takes provisional measures until the threat is overcome. It may depart from the principle of economic freedom, if deemed necessary.

Article 49 Structural Policy

The Commonwealth may support economically threatened regions and promote sectors of the economy and professions if such measures protect the Commonwealth interest. It may depart from the principle of economic freedom, if deemed necessary.

Article 50 Agriculture

(1) Legislation regarding agriculture is a Satrapial matter unless certain agricultural practices have intersatrapial consequences. Then the Commonwealth may legislate on such matters.

(2) The Commonwealth shall prohibit agricultural practices and products that are shown through research to be harmful to human health, soil and groundwater health, or the environment in general, throughout the Guarded Domains.

(3) Both Commonwealth and Satrapies shall create policies to promote sustainable agricultural practices.

Article 51 Alcohol

(1) Licensing on the production, the refining, and the sale of alcohol is a Satrapial matter.

(2) Legislation prohibiting or limiting alcohol production, refining, sales, or consumption by individuals 18 or older is prohibited.

(3) No child may purchase or consume alcohol.

Article 52 Recreational Drugs

(1) The licensing of recreational drug production and sales is a Satrapial matter.

(2) Legislation prohibiting or limiting recreational drug production, sales, or consumption by individuals 18 or older is prohibited.

(3) Recreational drugs that research finds increase violent behavior in individuals may be subject to higher regulation.

(4) No child may purchase or use recreational drugs.

Article 53 Prostitution

(1) Licensing of prostitution and brothels is a Satrapial matter.

(2) Government shall not prohibit individuals from selling sexual services.

(3) Government shall not prohibit individuals from buying sexual services.

(4) Individuals who sell sexual services shall be protected and regulated equally under the law.

(5) Children are prohibited from selling sexual services or buying sexual services.

Article 54 Gambling

(1) The licensing of gambling establishments is a Satrapial matter.

(2) Government shall not prohibit gambling or lotteries.

Article 55 Weapons and Military Material

(1) The Commonwealth legislates on the use of weapons, associated equipment, and ammunition.

(2) It legislates on the production, acquisition, distribution, importation, exportation, and transit of armaments and military and surveillance technologies.

Section 8 Housing, Work, Social Security and Health

Article 56 Landlord and Tenant

(1) The Satrapies shall legislate against abuses between landlord and tenant. They shall protect tenants against abusive rent, unreasonable notices of termination, and on the limited extension of tenancies.

(2) They may legislate to confer generally binding effect on contracts between landlords and tenants, including contracts made prior to the law. Contracts may become generally binding only if they respect the principle of equality before the law, and fairly take into account the justified interests of minority groups and regional differences.

Article 57 Labor

The Satrapies may legislate on:

a. the protection of employees against exploitation;

b. employee and employer relations;

c. placement services;

d. collective labor contracts

e. worksite safety.

Article 58 Employee Pension Plans

(1) The Satrapies may legislate on employee pension plans, or old age, survivors', and disability insurance.

Article 59 Unemployment Insurance

The Satrapies may legislate on unemployment insurance.

Article 60 Assistance to Needy Individuals

The Satrapies may assist needy individuals within their jurisdictions. The Commonwealth may support the Satrapies if support is requested.

Article 61 Family Support

(1) The Satrapies may support measures to protect the family. In fulfilling their tasks, they shall take into account the needs of the family.

(2) They may legislate on family allocations.

(3) They may legislate on paid maternity and paternity leave.

(4) They may legislate on affordable childcare.

Article 62 Health and Accident Insurance

The Commonwealth legislates on private health and accident insurance.

Article 63 Protection of Health

(1) The Commonwealth shall take measures for the protection of human health.

(2) It shall legislate on:

a. food safety;

b. the use of therapeutics, drugs, supplements, organisms, chemicals, objects, and practices which may be dangerous to health;

b. preventing and fighting communicable and noncommunicable human and animal diseases;

d. health promotion for the general public.

Article 64 Universal Healthcare[47]

(1) The Commonwealth shall create a single payer healthcare system for the Guarded Domains of Iranshahr.

(2) No child or individual shall be excluded from this healthcare system.

(3) The healthcare system shall take the best traits from successful healthcare systems around the world. In particular, it shall prioritize disease prevention measures over disease treatment.

(4) Sufficient resources shall be allocated to the following preventative measures:

a. Health promotion

b. Immunization

c. Family planning

d. Sexual and reproductive health

e. Disease screenings

f. Annual mental health screenings

g. Annual physical health screenings

Article 65 Medical Assistance to Procreation and Human Gene Technology

(1) Individuals shall be protected against the abuse of gene technology and medically assisted procreation.

(2) The Commonwealth shall legislate on the use of human reproductive and genetic material using the following principles:

a. The cloning of humans shall be prohibited. The cloning of human organs for the purpose of surgical transplanting shall be strictly regulated;

---

[47] T. R Reid, *The Healing of America: A Global Quest for Better, Cheaper, and Fairer Health Care   : [With an Explanation of the 2010 Health Reform Bill* (New York: Penguin Books, 2010).

b. Genetic modification of human reproductive cells and embryos for the exclusive purpose of preventing rare diseases shall be strictly regulated. All other forms of genetic modifications in humans is prohibited;

b. Genetic modifications of human reproductive material with animal or plant reproductive and genetic material is prohibited;

c. Only in cases when sterility or the danger of transmission of a serious disease cannot be avoided, may methods of medically assisted procreation be used. Using medically assisted procreation in order to induce certain attributes in the fetus or to conduct research is prohibited. The fertilization of human ova outside the uterus shall be permitted for scientific research relating to disease treatment;

f. An individual's genetic material may only be analyzed, registered, or disclosed with the consent of that individual;

g. Every individual shall have access to the data concerning their ancestry;

h. A human who is considered genetically modified shall have the same rights as an individual and shall not be excluded from the possibility of attaining citizenship within the Guarded Domains.

Article 66 Transplantation Medicine

(1) The Commonwealth shall regulate the transplantation of human organs, tissue, and cells. It thereby protects human dignity, personality, and health.

(2) In particular, the Commonwealth establishes criteria for the fair assignment of organs.

(3) Donations of human organs, tissue, and cells are pro bono. The trade of human organs is prohibited.

Article 67 Non-Human Gene Technology

(1) The Commonwealth shall protect individuals and the environment against abuse of gene technology.

(2) The Commonwealth legislates on the use of non-human organism reproductive and genetic materials. It shall take into account the dignity of naturally selected genes in all organisms. It shall promote the security of humans and the environment and shall protect the genetic diversity of non-human species.

(3) Genetic modifications that induce organisms to produce chemicals that may harm humans or the environment are prohibited from use.

Section 9 Residence and Domicile of Foreigners

Article 68 General Provisions

(1) The Commonwealth legislates on immigration, emigration, on granting asylum, and residence and domicile of foreigners.

(2) Foreigners who endanger the Guarded Domains of Iranshahr's security may be removed from the Guarded Domains by force.

Section 10 Civil and Criminal Law, Weights and Measures

Article 69 Civil Law
(1) Legislation in the field of civil law and civil procedure is both a Commonwealth and Satrapial matter.
(2) The organization of the judiciary and civil justice are Satrapial matters, unless otherwise provided by statute.
(3) Civil law shall not be based on religious law.

Article 70 Criminal Law
(1) The Commonwealth legislates the principles of criminal law and criminal procedure.
(2) The Satrapies organize the judiciary, criminal justice, and execution of criminal penalties and measures, unless otherwise provided by statute.
(3) The Commonwealth may provide financial assistance to the Satrapies for:
a. the establishment of institutions relating to criminal justice;
b. the improvement of correctional facilities;
c. institutions conducting preventative measures regarding at-risk children and young individuals.
(4) Criminal law shall not be based on religious law.

Article 71 Ill Acquired Evidence
(1) Evidence acquired without a warrant shall not be ruled out from use in a court of law.
(2) A peace officer who illegally attains such evidence shall no longer serve as a peace officer.

Article 72 Administration of Prisons
(1) The administration of prisons is a Satrapial matter.
(2) Prisoners shall have weekly sessions with psychologists and group therapy.
(3) All food, clothing, utilities, and other necessary items shall be paid for in time worked by each prisoner.
(4) Prisoners shall not be forced to work. Compensation for labor shall be based on the minimum wage set by the Satrapy in which the prison is located.
(5) Prisons shall not be privately owned or operated by a business.

Article 73 Correctional Measures for Particularly Dangerous Criminals

(1) A perpetrator of sexual or other violent crimes who is qualified by expert testimony to be unable to reform through therapy and to pose a continued high risk of repeat offenses may be imprisoned for life without a chance of early release or temporary leave.

(2) If new scientific facts establish that the criminal can successfully be reformed through therapy and is no longer at risk of repeat offenses, their case can be reviewed for sentence adjustments. In the event that the individual is released due to new expert testimony, the administrative agency responsible for the release is liable for any repeat offences the individual commits.

(3) All expert testimony regarding perpetrators of such crimes must be presented by at least two independent and experienced human behavior experts on the basis of all relevant facts.

Article 74 Aid to Victims of Criminal Acts
The Commonwealth and the Satrapies shall provide assistance and appropriate compensation to victims of violent criminal acts who suffer financial difficulties due to physical, mental, and sexual harm endured.

Article 75 Weights and Measures
Legislation on weights and measures is a Commonwealth matter.

Article 76 Patent Law
(1) Legislation on patent law is a Commonwealth matter.
(2) Any material including chemical compounds that can be found in nature shall not be patented.
(3) Patent rights shall expire five years after the first product is sold on the market.

Section 11 Taxation and Basic Income

Article 77 Divisions of Taxation Power
(1) Taxation of individuals and corporations is a Satrapial matter.
(2) Taxation of the Satrapies is a Commonwealth matter.

Article 78 Commonwealth Taxation Powers
(1) The Commonwealth may use the following forms of taxation:
a. Proportional taxation may be levied on all revenue generated by the Satrapies. Such taxation shall not exceed fifty percent of a Satrapy's revenue.
b. Environmental taxation may be levied on Satrapies that have policies that scientific research has shown are damaging to the environment or human health. Such taxation shall not exceed five percent of a Satrapy's revenue.

c. War taxation may be levied on the Satrapies if the Commonwealth has need of emergency funds in times of war. Such taxation shall not exceed 25 percent of a Satrapy's revenue.

d. Financial transaction taxes may be levied on all individuals and businesses that use financial services.

(2) The Commonwealth may place tariffs on goods entering the Guarded Domains of Iranshahr.

(3) The Commonwealth may oblige the Satrapies to raise taxes on specific goods that may be detrimental to human or environmental health. The Commonwealth must show valid research to support such raises in taxes.

Article 79 Legal Forms of Satrapial Taxation

(1) The following are legal forms of taxation:

a. Proportional or progressive income taxes may be levied on individuals. Capital gains shall be included as a form of income.

b. Corporate taxes may be levied.

c. Value added taxes may be levied.

d. Sales taxes may be levied.

e. Excise taxes may be levied.

f. License fees may be levied.

g. Environmental taxes may be levied.

h. Tolls may be levied. Satrapial tolls may not be levied on individuals travelling on the Commonwealth highways.

i. Progressive consumption taxes may be levied on tap water in excess of an individual's basic water needs.

Article 80 Prohibited Forms of Taxation

(1) The following forms of taxation are prohibited:

a. Regressive income taxes.

b. Wealth taxes.

c. Property taxes.

d. Inheritance taxes.

e. Expatriation taxes.

f. Transfer taxes.

g. Poll taxes.

h. Jizya.

i. Sales taxes on non-processed food products and tap water.

Article 81 Legal Forms of Commonwealth Taxation

(1) The following are legal forms of taxation the Commonwealth may collect:

a. Proportional tax on Satrapial, Independent Shahrestan, and Vassal State income

b. Customs and duties on imported goods

c. Tolls on Commonwealth Highways for the maintenance of transportation infrastructure

(2) The Commonwealth may mandate the Satrapies, Independent Shahrestans, and Vassal States to collect a sustainability excise tax on goods and services that are found through scientific research to cause harm to individuals and/or to the environment.

Article 82 Measures Against Tax Avoidance

(1) All forms of tax deductions shall be prohibited.

(2) All forms of tax exemptions shall be prohibited.

(3) All tax returns submitted to the Commonwealth and the Satrapies shall be made available to the public.

Article 83 Dispensation of Basic Incomes[48]

(1) A basic income for every citizen shall be financed and dispensed by the Commonwealth.

(2) A basic income for every child shall be financed and dispensed by the Commonwealth to the parent or guardian of the child.

(3) The Satrapies may create Satrapial basic incomes for their citizens or resident individuals if they so choose.

CHAPTER 3 FINANCES AND CENSUS

Article 1 Budget

(1) All governments must maintain a balanced budget.

(2) If a government accumulates a deficit, it shall have one year to rebalance its budget.

(3) If a government should not balance its budget by the end of the five-year period, automatic cuts to the budget shall be enforced. A percent reduction to all parts of the budget shall be implemented each year until the budget is balanced.

---

[48] Daniel/ Wark Ravents. Julie, *Against Charity.* (Consortium Book Sales & Dist, 2018).

Article 2 Transparency

All budgets shall be published on the internet and in print so that any citizen may view and understand where their taxes are spent.

Article 3 Commonwealth Census

(1) The administration of a Commonwealth census is a Commonwealth matter.

(2) The Commonwealth census shall be administered every ten years.

(3) Census data shall be made publicly available.

TITLE 3 STRUCTURE OF THE COMMONWEALTH GOVERNMENT

CHAPTER 1 DIVISION OF COMMONWEALTH POWER

Article 1 Check and Balances
The Commonwealth Government shall be divided into independent branches. Checks and balances shall be placed so that no one branch may hold too much power.

Article 2 Divisions
The Commonwealth Government shall have the following branches:
(1) Legislative branch divided into two councils
(2) Judicial branch divided into two councils
(3) Executive branch
(4) The Central Bank of Iranshahr
(5) Bureau of Anti-Corruption
(6) The People

Article 3 Names of Institutions

(1) The upper house of the Legislature shall be called the Farrahan.[49]

(2) The lower house of the Legislature shall be called the Majlis.

(3) The upper chamber of the Judiciary shall be called the Supreme Court.

(4) The lower chamber of the Judiciary shall be called the Commonwealth Court.

(5) The head of the Executive branch shall be called the Vakil.[50]

(6) The heads of Executive Departments shall be called Divans.

Article 4 Service

(1) All members of the Commonwealth shall remember that they are the servants of the People of the Guarded Domains of Iranshahr.

(2) Power is entrusted to the Commonwealth by the People to empower, protect, and serve the interests of the People.

Article 5 Age of Service

(1) The age span in which a citizen may serve in the Commonwealth government, whatever the position, is from age 18 to age 75.

(2) A public servant who reaches the age of 75 shall retire from their position within thirty days after their birthday.

CHAPTER 2 LEGISLATIVE BRANCH

Section 1 General Functions

---

[49] The word "Farrahan" is a creation. In essence, it is supposed to mean "those with the farr," since these representatives are chosen by lottery (fortune or luck).

[50] John R. Perry, *Karīm Khān Zand: A History of Iran, 1747-1779*, Publications of the Center for Middle Eastern Studies ; No. 12 (Chicago: University of Chicago Press, 1979). I was drawn to the title *Vakil*, after reading about Karim Khan Zand's use of the title instead of *Shah* or *Shahanshah*. This term in its original use meant "the people's representative" which makes sense why in modern use it means "lawyer."

Article 1 Role of the Legislature

The Commonwealth Legislature is the embodiment of the People. It shall be composed of an upper house and a lower house.

Article 2 Powers

The Legislature is granted the following powers:

(1) Create bills for judicial review.

(2) Vote on legislation presented to it by the People, the Executive Branch, and members of the Legislature.

(3) Ratify treaties with regional and international actors.

(4) Approve Executive appointees to departments of the Executive Branch.

Article 3 Creating Legislation

(1) The Majlis shall create legislation for review by the Commonwealth Judges.

(2) Legislation shall be concise, easily read and reviewed, and shall be organized into clearly defined sections.

(3) If proposed legislation is found unconstitutional, it shall be returned to the Majlis for correction of sections that are deemed unconstitutional.

(4) After corrections are made, the proposed legislation is resent to the Commonwealth Judges.

Article 4 Passing Legislation

(1) If the Commonwealth Judges find the proposed legislation constitutional, the Farrahan shall vote on the proposed legislation.

(2) The Farrahan shall review and vote on each section of the proposed legislation.

(3) Should part or all of the proposed legislation fail to attain a majority vote, the Farrahan shall propose revisions for the Majlis.

(4) The Majlis shall revise the sections of the proposed legislation using the proposed revisions from the Farrahan, or it shall propose new revisions.

(5) Once revisions are made, the proposed legislation is sent to the Commonwealth Judges and the process begins anew.

Article 5 Treaties

Treaties that do not limit sovereignty shall be voted on by both houses. A majority in both houses must occur for treaty ratification.

Article 6 Executive Appointees

The Vakil may appoint Divans with the majority consent of both Farrahan and Majlis.

Article 7 Overriding Executive Veto

If 60 percent of the Farrahan votes to pass a bill, an Executive veto will have no power.

Section 2 Structure

Article 8 Bicameral Legislature

The Legislature shall be composed of Farrahan and Majlis.

Article 9 Farrahan

(1) The Farrahan shall be composed of two citizens, one female and one male, called Farrahani, from each Satrapy in the Guarded Domains.[51]

(2) Each member of the Farrahan shall serve a single term of three years.

(3) Each Farrahani shall receive a salary of 100 Darics per annum at the expense of the Commonwealth.

(4) Lodging shall be given to a Farrahani and their dependents at the expense of the Commonwealth.

Article 10 Majlis

(1) The Majlis shall be composed of citizens called Majlisi, each representing 50,000 citizens of the Satrapy of domicile.

(2) Each Majlisi may serve up to four terms. Each term shall be three years.

(3) Each year one third of the Majlisi seats shall be up for election.

(4) Each Majlisi shall receive a salary of no more than 100 Darics per annum at the expense of the Satrap.

(5) Lodging shall be given to a Majlisi and their dependents at the expense of the Commonwealth.

Section 3 Selection

Article 11 Farrahan Selection

(1) A citizen of the Guarded Domains of Iranshahr is eligible for selection to the Farrahan.

---

[51] Anja Flach Michael Knapp and Ercan Ayboga, *Revolution in Rojava Democratic Autonomy and Women's Liberation in Syrian Kurdistan* (Pluto Press, 2016). In Syrian towns governed by the Syrian Democratic Forces, there are two mayors, one female and one male.

(2) Each Farrahani shall be chosen by lottery from among the citizenry of the Satrapy. Selection by lottery will occur until one female citizen and one male citizen have been chosen.[52]

(3) Selection of a new Farrahani shall be one year and six months before the end of the old Farrahani's term.

(4) The Farrahani-elect may refuse participation but shall be strongly urged to serve.

(5) The Farrahani-elect shall have six months to make arrangements before moving to the Capital of the Guarded Domains.

(6) The Farrahani-elect shall receive one year of training on the processes of the Farrahan prior to participation. Training shall entail shadowing current Farrahanis of the Farrahani's Satrapy of domicile.

Article 12 Majlisi Selection

(1) A citizen who has passed the Commonwealth Basics Test may run for the Majlis.

(2) Each Satrapy shall have a Majlisi for every 50,000 citizens domiciled in the Satrapy.

(2) Each Majlisi shall be elected through open-party list ballot proportional representation in the Satrapy of domicile.

(3) The Majlisi-elect shall have three months to make arrangements before moving to the Capital of the Guarded Domains.

(4) The Majlisi-elect shall receive nine months of training on the processes of the Majlis prior to participation. Training shall entail shadowing current Majlisi of the Majlisi-elect's Satrapy of domicile.

---

[52] John P. McCormick, *Machiavellian Democracy* (Cambridge, [England]; New York: Cambridge University Press, 2011). The use of lottery in ancient and medieval republics like Venice were meant prevent corruption that can occur in elections. My interest in using a lottery system for this political office is to ensure that average citizens participate in government. Even in a democratic society, political classes form from almost exclusively privileged families. Lottery ensures that at least part of the Commonwealth government reflects the makeup of the People.

CHAPTER 3 JUDICIAL BRANCH

Section 1 General Functions

Article 1 General Role of the Judiciary
The Judiciary Branch of the Commonwealth ensures that laws created by the Commonwealth Legislature and Satrapial Legislatures are constitutional.

Article 2 Commonwealth Court
(1) Commonwealth Court shall receive each bill created by Majlis and determine whether every section of that bill is constitutional. Should one or more sections of a bill be determined as unconstitutional, the Judges shall return the bill to Majlis with clear and concise reasons why one or more sections are unconstitutional. Majlis shall make amendments to the bill and resubmit for judicial review.

(3) Propositions with the proper number of citizen signatures submitted by the People shall be reviewed by the Commonwealth Court in the same manner as with Majlis.

(4) The Judges shall review treaties to determine whether they are constitutional. If a treaty is unconstitutional, the Judges shall give clear and concise reasons why it is unconstitutional. If a treaty is constitutional, the Judges shall determine if the Commonwealth Legislature must ratify it or the People.

(5) All judgments must be made within three months of receiving documents for review.

(6) Each judge shall have one vote when determining the constitutionality of a section of a bill, proposition, or treaty.

(7) The majority decision shall determine the constitutionality of the document in question.

Article 3 Supreme Court
(1) The Supreme Court shall be the highest court in the Guarded Domains.

(2) Supreme Judges shall receive appeals cases from citizens or Satrapies concerning laws and judgments deemed unjust or unconstitutional.

(3) Citizens or Satrapies must appeal to all lower levels of judges before appealing to the Supreme Judges.

(4) All judgments must be made within one year of receiving appeal case.

(5) Once a judgment is made all similar cases in the Guarded Domains must be judged similarly by lower courts.

Section 2 Structure

Article 4 Commonwealth Court Organization

(1) The Commonwealth Court shall be composed of seven citizen judges.

(2) Each Judge shall serve one term of seven years.

(3) A new Judge shall be selected every year. As one Judge finishes their term, a new one is chosen. If a Judge should die before their term is finished, a new Judge shall be selected to serve the duration of the term.

(4) Each Judge shall receive a salary of 100 Darics per annum at the expense of the Commonwealth.

(5) Lodging shall be given to a Judge and their dependents at the expense of the Commonwealth.

Article 5 Supreme Court Organization

(1) The Supreme Court shall be composed of seven citizen judges.

(2) Each Judge shall serve one term of seven years.

(3) A new Judge shall be selected every year. As one Judge finishes their term, a new one is chosen. If a Judge should die before their term is finished, a new Judge shall be selected to serve the duration of the term.

(4) Each Judge shall receive a salary of 100 Darics per annum at the expense of the Commonwealth.

(5) Lodging shall be given to a Judge and their dependents at the expense of the Commonwealth.

Section 3 Selection

Article 6 Judiciary Eligibility

(1) A citizen who has acquired a doctorate in the School of Judges is eligible for selection to serve in the judiciary. Recent graduates shall be eligible to apply for the lowest level courts.

(2) Each Judge shall be selected by lottery from a pool of judges from the lower court. At each level of the judiciary, judges will be eligible for selection to the next higher court level after serving a minimum of two years in their current court.

(3) Each Judge-elect may refuse participation but shall be strongly urged to serve.

(4) Each Judge-elect shall have three months to make arrangements before moving to the location of the court in which they will serve.

(5) Each Judge-elect shall receive three months of training on the processes of the Judiciary prior to participation. Training shall entail shadowing current Judges.

CHAPTER 4 EXECUTIVE BRANCH

Section 1 General Functions

Article 1 Head of the Executive Branch
(1) The head of the Commonwealth Executive Branch shall be the Vakil.
(2) Appointed by the Vakil are the Divans who shall head the departments of the Commonwealth Executive branch.

Article 2 Head of State
The Vakil shall represent the Guarded Domains of Iranshahr in the international sphere.

Article 3 Commander in Chief
(1) The Vakil shall be the Commander in Chief of the military forces of the Guarded Domains of Iranshahr.
(2) With the majority consent of the Farrahan, the Vakil may declare war to protect citizens harmed abroad, protect allies, or protect oppressed peoples asking for assistance from the Guarded Domains.

Article 3 Enforcer
The Vakil and the Divans shall enforce the laws that the Legislature passes to the fullest extent of their powers and resources.

Article 4 Veto Power
The Vakil may veto a bill. If the veto is not overruled with 60 percent of the Farrahan vote on the bill in question, the Vakil may return the bill to Majlis with specific corrections that the Vakil would find sufficient. Majlis do not have to use the corrections suggested.

Article 5 Suggestions for Legislature
The Vakil may submit recommendations for legislation to Majlis or may create outline bills for Majlis to modify.

Article 6 Appointments
The Vakil may appoint the following officials with a majority support from the Legislature:
a. Divans

b. Diplomats

Article 7 Law Giver
The Vakil shall sign into law bills and treaties passed by the Legislature or the People.

Article 8 General Functions of the Vazir-e Azam
(1) The Vazir-e Azam is the successor of the Vakil should the Vakil die, resign from office, or be impeached by the Majlis or the People.

(2) The Vazir-e Azam shall be an advisor to the Vakil should the Vakil require council.

(3) The Vazir-e Azam may cast one vote in the Farrahan if the Farrahan vote is tied.

(4) The Vakil may assign duties to the Vazir-e Azam at their discretion.

Article 9 General Functions of the Divans
(1) The Divans shall head the departments assigned to them by the Vakil.

(2) The Divans shall execute laws relevant to their departments.

(3) The Divans shall sit at the Council.

(4) The role of the Council is to advise the Vakil on any subject requiring the Vakil's attention.

(5) A Divan shall not head more than one department and shall not interfere in other departments.

Section 2 Structure

Article 10 Office of Vakil
(1) The office of Vakil shall be composed of a single citizen.

(2) The Vakil may serve up to two terms, each term being six years. More than two terms is strictly forbidden.

(3) The Vakil shall receive a salary from the Commonwealth of no more than 250 darics per annum.

(4) Lodging shall be given to the Vakil and their dependents at the expense of the Commonwealth.

Article 11 Office of Vazir-e Azam
(1) The office of Vazir-e Azam shall be composed of a single citizen appointed by the Vakil.

(2) The Vazir-e Azam shall serve as long as the Vakil is in office or as long as the Vakil keeps the Vazir-e Azam.

(3) The Vazir-e Azam shall receive a salary from the Commonwealth of no more than 150 darics per annum.

(4) Lodging shall be given to the Vazir-e Azam and their dependents at the expense of the Commonwealth.

Article 12 The Divans

(1) The Divans shall be composed of one citizen per department.

(2) Each Divan shall be responsible for one of the following departments:

a. Health

b. Environment

c. Justice

d. Resource Management

e. Development

f. Treasury

g. Foreign Affairs

h. Military

i. Commerce

j. Research and Development

(3) Each Divan shall serve as long as the Vakil is in office or until the Vakil replaces them.

(4) Each Divan shall receive a salary from the Commonwealth of no more than 150 darics per annum.

(5) Lodging shall be given to a Divan and their dependents at the expense of the Commonwealth.

Section 3 Selection

Article 13 Eligibility

(1) Eligibility for serving as Vakil is as follows:

a. Must be a citizen.

b. Must pass the Commonwealth Basics Test.

c. Has never been found guilty of corruption.

(2) A citizen running for the office of Vakil must choose another citizen to be their candidate for Vazir-e Azam.

Article 14 Election of the Vakil

(1) The election of the Vakil shall go through two votes.

(2) The citizens shall vote for their preferred candidate. The two candidates with the highest number of votes shall be the winners of the first vote.

(3) The first vote shall take place one year before the end of the current Vakil's term.

(4) Three months following the first vote, citizens shall vote between the two remaining candidates. The candidate with the highest number of votes shall serve as Vakil.

Article 15 Preparations for Office
The Vakil-elect shall have nine months to organize their Council and present the candidates for Divan offices to the Majlis.

Article 16 Oath of the Vakil
(1) Upon taking office, the Vakil-elect shall recite the Oath before the People.
(2) While reciting the Oath, the Vakil-elect shall raise one hand and place the other on an object or individual sacred to the Vakil-elect.
(3) The Oath shall be recited as follows:

"I, (name) am the servant of the Guarded Domains of Iranshahr and its sovereign, the People of Iranshahr. I swear upon my honor and this (name of object or individual) that I will defend the Constitution and the People, from foreign and domestic threats. I shall not forsake the many for the few, nor shall I oppress the few by the command of the many. I shall resist the temptations of power and put the wellbeing and prosperity of the People before all else. I accept the Farr from the Simorgh knowing that it is not mine to keep but to use to honor the past, improve the present, and protect the future."

CHAPTER 5 CENTRAL BANK OF IRANSHAHR

Section 1 General Functions

Article 1 Powers
(1) The Central Bank of Iranshahr shall have the following powers:
a. Implement monetary policies.
b. Determine interest rates for the Guarded Domains.
c. Regulate and supervise the banking industry.

d. Control the Guarded Domains's supply of money.

e. Act as the banker of last resort.

f. Manage the Guarded Domains's inflation, exchange rate, gold reserves, Commonwealth stock register, and foreign exchange rate.

g. Work with the Legislature and the Vakil to create policies that bring prosperity to the People.

(2) The Central Bank of Iranshahr shall not create money that is not completely backed by gold bullion.

(3) Any policy made by the Central Bank of Iranshahr can be reversed by any of the following processes:

a. A simple majority in both Farrahan and Majlis.

b. A simple majority by the People in a General Referendum.

c. If the Judges of the Commonwealth find the policy to be unconstitutional.

d. If the Vakil vetoes the policy and the policy is not supported by five or more Central Bankers.

Article 2 Decision Making Process

(1) A policy shall take effect if four of the seven Central Bankers vote in favor of a policy.

(2) Policies can be created at the request of a Central Banker, the Legislature, or the Vakil.

Section 2 Structure

Article 3 Central Bankers

(1) The Central Bank of Iranshahr Board shall consist of seven citizens.

(2) Each Central Banker shall serve one term of six years. The Central Banker shall be divided into two groups; one consisting of three members and the other consisting of four members. These two groups shall be separated by three years of service as Central Banker. When the group of three is in the sixth year of its term, the group of four shall be in the third year of its term. When the group of four is in the sixth year of its term, the group of three shall be in the third year of its term.

(3) Each Central Banker shall receive a salary from the Commonwealth of no more than 150 darics per annum.

Section 3 Selection

Article 4 Eligibility for Central Banker Office

Any citizen that passes the Central Bank Examination and is chosen as the best candidate by Majlis may become a Central Banker.

Article 5 Central Bank Examination

(1) Majlis shall elect seven qualified Majlisi to create two exams to test applicants for the Board. The seven Majlisi may be advised by academic experts so long as the advisors do not take the exams and shall swear secrecy relating to the material of the exams.

(2) The first exam shall consist of 101 questions of great difficulty. 100 questions shall be objective. One question shall be a scenario on which the applicants shall write an essay explaining what they would do as a Central Banker. The questions shall relate to economics and financial institutions. The seven Majlisi shall choose the three top applicants. The names of all the applicants shall not be known to the Majlisi.

(3) The top three applicants shall then take a second exam consisting of three scenarios a Central Banker could face. The applicants shall write essays for each explaining how they would deal with each scenario. Majlis shall then vote on the best answer for each scenario, not knowing the names of the three applicants. The applicant with the best answers shall be elected to the office.

CHAPTER 6 BUREAU OF ANTI-CORRUPTION

Section 1 General Functions

Article 1 Powers

(1) The Bureau of Anti-Corruption shall have the following powers:

a. Randomly audit the branches of the Commonwealth for financial irregularities and corrupt practices.

b. Investigate all reported incidences of potentially corrupt behavior.

c. Investigate not just the suspect individual or organization, but also any individual or organization with ties to the suspect and to examine their financial and other records with a warrant.

d. Subpoena individuals for interview.

f. Refer to the Justice Department any potential criminal activities not related to corruption which is disclosed in the course of a corruption investigation.

Section 2 Structure

Article 2 Office of Censor[53]
(1) The office of Censor shall be composed of a single citizen.
(2) The Censor may serve up to two terms, each term being six years. More than two terms is strictly forbidden.
(3) The Censor shall receive a salary from the Commonwealth of no more than 200 darics per annum.
(4) Lodging shall be given to the Censor and their dependents at the expense of the Commonwealth.

Section 3 Selection

Article 3 Eligibility
The following are criterion for Censor Eligibility:
(1) A citizen of the Guarded Domains of Iranshahr
(2) Has had no criminal or civil convictions.
(3) Passes the Anti-Corruption Test.

Article 4 Election of the Censor
(1) The election of the Censor shall go through two votes.
(2) The citizens shall vote for their preferred candidate. The two candidates with the highest number of votes shall be the winners of the first vote.
(3) The first vote shall take place six months before the end of the current Censor's term.
(4) Three months following the first vote, citizens shall vote between the two remaining candidates. The candidate with the highest number of votes shall serve as Censor.

Article 7 Oath of the Censor
(1) Upon taking office, the Censor-elect shall recite the Oath before the People.

---

[53] Niccolò Machiavelli et al., *The Discourses [of] Niccolò Machiavelli* (Harmondsworth: Penguin, 1970). The censors of ancient Rome would regulate moral behavior of those in political office and the general public. The censor in this constitution is meant to root out corruption among all levels of the political system.

(2) While reciting the Oath, the Censor-elect shall raise one hand and place the other on an object or individual sacred to the Censor-elect.

(3) The Oath shall be recited as follows:

"I, (name) am the servant of the Guarded Domains of Iranshahr and its sovereign, the People of Iranshahr. I swear upon my honor and this (name of object or individual) that I will defend the Constitution and the People, from foreign and domestic threats. I shall be the eyes and ears of the People to uphold good governance. I shall use the office of Censor to root out corruption without bias, and I renounce affiliations with political parties and ideologies. This I swear.

CHAPTER 7 THE PEOPLE

Section 1 General Functions

Article 1 Sovereignty of the People
The People rule the Guarded Domains of Iranshahr. The will of the People shall supersede any political institution of the Commonwealth or the Satrapies.

Article 2 Voting Day
(1) The Commonwealth shall establish an annual holiday in which the People may vote on propositions.

(2) This annual holiday shall be called Voting Day.

(3) On Voting Day, propositions of all kinds shall be put before the General Referendum.

(4) Satrapial Referendums may also occur on Voting Day, or Satrapies can establish a different date to vote on Satrapial propositions.

Section 2 Powers

Article 3 Electing Officials
The People shall elect government officials according to the powers given by the Constitution.

Article 4 Propose Legislation to the People
(1) Citizens may create propositions for legislation.

(2) In order for a citizen's proposition to become law, the following must occur in order:

a. A proposition must acquire 250,000 different signatures of support within two years of the first signature of support.

b. A proposition must be deemed constitutional by the Judges of the Commonwealth.

c. A proposition must acquire a majority of the votes in favor of it becoming law.

(3) Any proposition that is not passed must wait a period of two years before the process can begin anew.

Article 5 Propose Legislation to the Farrahan

(1) A citizen may submit a proposition for legislation to the Farrahan for a vote.

(2) A proposition proposed to the Farrahan must follow the same procedure as the process to propose legislation to the People.

Article 6 Treaties

(1) All treaties that limit Commonwealth sovereignty must attain a majority of the votes by the People.

(2) A citizen may propose a treaty in the same manner as a proposition for legislation.

Article 7 Declare and End War

(1) The People may declare or end wars in which the Guarded Domains is engaged in.

(2) 250,000 different signatures are required within a two year time frame to propose either a declaration of war or a proposal ending a war.

(3) A majority vote in favor of a declaration of war requires the Commonwealth to declare war within three months of the vote.

(4) A majority vote in favor of ending a war requires the Commonwealth to end a war within three months of the vote.

Article 8 Removing Members of the Farrahan or Majlis

(1) A Farrahani or Majlisi may be removed from office by the citizens of the Satrapy they serve.

(2) 10,000 different signatures in support of such a proposition are required for a vote by the citizens of a Satrapy. Signatures must come from citizens domiciled in the official's Satrapy.

(3) A majority in favor of removing a Farrahani or Majlisi shall require the following:

a. A special election for a replacement Majlisi to serve out the remainder of the impeached Majlisi's term.

b. A special random selection for a replacement Farrahani to serve out the remainder of the impeached Farrahani's term.

Article 9 Major Recall

(1) The People may remove all members of the Farrahan, the Majlis, or the entire Legislature.

(2) To remove one branch of Legislature or both, 300,000 different signatures are required for the proposition to go to a vote.

(3) A majority vote in favor of such a proposition shall require the following to occur:

a. If the Farr is removed, special random selections shall occur in all Satrapies of the Guarded Domains. The replacement Farrahanis shall serve out the remainder of the impeached Farrahanis' terms.

b. If the Majlis is removed, special elections shall occur in all Satrapies of the Guarded Domains. The replacement Majlisi shall serve out the remainder of the impeached Majlisi's terms.

Article 10 Removing Other Officials

The People may remove any official from the Executive Branch, Judicial Branch, or the Central Bank of Iranshahr in the following manner:

(1) A proposition shall gather 250,000 different signatures supporting it.

(2) On Voting Day, the proposition shall go to a vote in the General Referendum.

(3) Should the proposition pass with a majority of the votes, the following shall happen:

a. If the Vakil is removed, the Vazir-e Azam shall serve as Vakil for the remainder of the term.

b. If any executive official below the Vakil is removed, the Vakil shall appoint a replacement official.

c. If a Judge is removed, a special random selection shall choose a replacement Judge to serve the remainder of the impeached Judge's term.

d. If a Central Banker is removed, the process of electing a Central Banker shall be implemented to find a replacement.

Article 11 Partial Constitutional Reform

(1) The People may amend the Commonwealth Constitution through a proposition supported by 500,000 different signatures acquired within a two year period.

(2) A proposition to amend the Commonwealth Constitution requires 60 percent of the votes in favor.

(3) An amendment shall take effect one year after approval.

Article 12 Full Constitutional Reform

(1) The People may require a new Constitution.

(2) Such a proposition shall require one million different citizen signatures. These signatures must be acquired within a five year period.

(3) Full constitutional reform requires 60 percent of the vote in favor.

Article 13 Half Century Reform[54]

(1) Every fifty years following the ratification of this Constitution, the People shall vote on whether to keep the Constitution or create a new one.

(2) If a simple majority decides to create a new Constitution, a Constitutional Convention shall convene six months after the vote.

(3) Legislatures from each Satrapy and Enclave shall send delegations to the Constitutional Convention to draft the new Constitution.

(4) Any citizen domiciled within the Satrapy or Enclave may apply to be a delegate for the Satrapy or Enclave. The applicant must receive two-thirds approval from the Satrapial or Enclave legislature to become a delegate. Each applicant shall receive equal treatment within the application process.

(5) Satrapial delegations shall have one vote for every Majlisi representing the Satrapy in the Commonwealth Majlis. Enclave delegations shall form one delegation bloc in which this bloc shall have one vote for every 50,000 people of the combined total Enclave populations based on the most recent census. Vassal States may send delegations but delegates shall have no votes.

(6) The completion of a draft Constitution requires two-thirds of the total delegation votes approval.

Article 14 Ratification of a New Constitution

(1) Six months after the drafting of the new Constitution, a second referendum shall be held, whereby citizens shall vote either for the draft Constitution or for the old Constitution.

---

[54] Thomas Jefferson and Barbara Oberg, *The Papers of Thomas Jefferson* (Princeton, N.J.; Woodstock: Princeton University Press, 2008). Jefferson mused about the need for constitutions to be reformed or remade every so often. Whether he was serious about the idea or not, I find it to be a good idea that the People should renew their "social contract." Voting every 50 years on the legitimacy of the political system will create a renewed sense of ownership over their political system.

(2) A draft Constitution must be ratified by two-thirds of voters to become the new Constitution of the Guarded Domains of Iranshahr.

(3) If the draft Constitution receives a simple majority under two-thirds of the total vote, the draft Constitution shall be sent back to the Constitutional Convention for modification. The revised draft Constitution shall then be put to a new referendum.

(4) A draft Constitution that receives less that fifty percent of the vote is defeated, and the old Constitution shall stand as the Constitution of the Guarded Domains of Iranshahr for the next fifty years.

TITLE 4 TOPICS OF GREAT IMPORTANCE

CHAPTER 1 CITIZEN'S SERVICE[55]

Section 1 Purpose

Article 1 Principle
Citizen's Service is a rigorous education in civic virtues for individuals wishing to become citizens. It shall not be indoctrination but a republican training giving individuals the tools to exercise their political rights and duties.

Article 2 Republican Education[56]

---

[55] Plato and Desmond Lee, *Plato: The Republic* (London: Penguin, 2003). The idea for Citizen's Service came from Plato's idea of taking select children to train as a specialized political elite who would then rule the republic. As Plato's actual idea is unethical and antidemocratic in my opinion, my aim is to democratize his idea. By bringing all the young people of Iranshahr into one place, away from their communities, they can be trained in the art of civic virtue, and help reduce prejudice between different ethnicities and faiths by creating assabiyah and new friendships.

[56] Philip Pettit, *Republicanism: A Theory of Freedom and Government*, Oxford Political Theory (Oxford : New York: Clarendon Press ; Oxford University Press, 1997).

Citizen's Service shall teach the individual about the Constitution and the political rights and duties it provides the individual. The individual shall be taught what citizenship offers in responsibilities and benefits.

Article 3 Military Training

The individual shall receive basic military training and conditioning.

Article 4 Health and Nutrition

Citizen's Service shall provide an education in nutrition and preventative health for the individual.

Article 5 Debate and Discussion

The individual shall learn how to debate political issues and shall discuss topics with instructors and peers in forum settings.

Article 6 Exposure

The individual shall congregate with other individuals from every corner of the Guarded Domains. The individual will live with, learn with, debate with, and train with individuals of different ethnicities, languages, traditions, religions, classes, and sexes.

Article 7 Mental Health Initiative

Every individual shall spend a minimum of three sessions with mental health professionals. Individuals in need shall receive more sessions as the mental health professional determines necessary.

Article 8 Physical Health Initiative

Every individual shall undergo a physical health examination by health professionals to help individuals understand and manage their health.

Section 2 Citizen's Service Structure

Article 9 Process

Every individual shall attend Citizen's Service one month following graduation from primary education. Citizen's Service is mandatory to receive both citizenship and a primary education diploma.

Article 10 Duration of Citizen's Service

Citizen's Service shall be divided into four quarters, each quarter consisting of three full months.

Article 11 Citizen's City

(1) The Commonwealth shall establish and manage a permanent compound secluded from all other cities, towns, or villages. It shall be called the Citizen's City.

(2) On its premises there shall be housing, a hospital, a dining commons, a library, classrooms, and training fields.

Article 12 Bare Essentials

(1) The individual shall receive clothing, food, shelter, and needed medication in the Citizen's City.

(2) Any personal belongings are prohibited in the Citizen's City. Exceptions are made for medically necessary equipment.

(3) Prohibited items shall be placed into storage until the individual completes Citizen's Service.

Article 13 Classes Taken

(1) Classes shall be taught coed.

(2) Classes shall be structured so that individuals may discuss topics with instructors and fellow classmates.

(3) Attendance is mandatory.

(4) Military training shall consist of the following:

a. Gun safety and use

b. Team-based exercises

c. Balance, self-control, and stress management training

d. Endurance and strength training.

(5) Academic classes shall consist of:

a. Constitution Studies

b. Health and Nutrition

c. Personal Finance

d. Rhetoric, Debate, Integrative Negotiation

c. Social Justice

Article 14 Living Quarters

(1) Living quarters shall be segregated by gender.

(2) Beds shall be allotted at random to increase diversity of roommates.

Section 3 Graduation

Article 15 Citizenship

Upon finishing the 12 months of Citizen's Service, the individual shall be granted the title Citizen and all the rights and responsibilities that come with such a title.

Article 14 Citizen Number
The individual shall receive a ten-digit identification number. With this number, the citizen can access their benefits and fulfill their duties.

CHAPTER 2 SECESSION AND EXPANSION

Section 1 Secession

Article 1 Right of a People
The right for a region to secede shall be guaranteed.

Article 2 Satrapial Secession
If 60 percent of the People domiciled in a Satrapy vote to secede, the Satrapy shall secede from the Guarded Domains one year after the vote.

Article 3 Shahrestan Secession
If 60 percent of the People domiciled in a Shahrestan vote to secede from its Satrapy, the Shahrestan shall secede from the Satrapy one year after the vote.

Article Citizenship and Secession
Any citizen of the Guarded Domains who applies for citizenship in a newly independent state resulting from secession must forfeit their citizenship status in the Guarded Domains.

Section 2 Expansion

Article 4 Guarded Domains' Expansion
If more than fifty percent of voting individuals in a territory outside the borders of the Guarded Domains vote to join the Guarded Domains, the territory shall be annexed one year after the vote.

Article 5 Satrapial Expansion
(1) If 60 percent of the People domiciled in a Shahrestan vote to join a Satrapy, the Satrapy shall annex the Shahrestan one year after the vote.

(2) If 60 percent of the People domiciled in a Shahrestan vote to create a new Satrapy with other willing Shahrestans, the merger shall take place one year after the vote.

CHAPTER 3 TOPICS IN THE DOMESTIC SPHERE

Section 1 Electronic Citizen's Forum[57]

Article 1 Purpose

(1) The Commonwealth shall establish an Electronic Citizen's Forum in which every citizen may give their opinion on various political topics at the Commonwealth, Satrapy, and Shahrestan level.

(2) The Electronic Citizen's Forum shall give politicians information about the will of their constituents.

Article 2 Structure

(1) Every citizen shall use their Citizen Number to create a confidential profile.

(2) This profile shall allow the citizen to access the Commonwealth site and the sites of the citizen's Satrapy and Shahrestan of domicile.

(3) The citizen's profile shall have the following optional features:

a. Political party preference

b. Social values

c. Political values

d. Most important political issues

e. Socio-economic status, ethnicity, gender, religion, sexual orientation

---

[57] Dagger, *Civic Virtues*. Dagger writes about the potential of internet voting to increase voting in general. Living in a world where countries and actors can sway elections or even hack voting machines, I do not think this is a good idea. However, having a digital space where citizens can voice their concerns on issues and where public officials can get a sense of public opinion would enhance the political process.

Article 3 Electronic Citizen's Forum Site Activities

(1) The citizen may do the following activities on the Commonwealth Site:

a. Rate any branch of the Commonwealth government

b. Rate public servants

c. Rate proposed bills

d. Rate judgments

e. Rate proposed treaties

f. Rate propositions

(2) Any activity shall give the option of approve, disapprove, or abstain. For every activity, the citizen's default answer shall be abstain until the citizen changes their answer.

(3) Commonwealth public officials may pose questions to the site for citizen feedback.

(4) The citizen may pose questions or support questions from other citizens to particular public officials or to fellow citizens.

Article 4 Satrapy and Shahrestan Sites

The sites of the Satrapies and Shahrestans shall have similar activities to the Commonwealth Site for their regional and local issues.

Section 2 Natural Wealth Management

Article 5 Possession of the People

All natural wealth within the Guarded Domains of Iranshahr belongs to the People as a whole.

Article 6 Natural Wealth Definition

Natural wealth shall include fossil fuels, precious and nonprecious metals, precious stones, forests, coastlines, and industrial nonmetals.

Article 7 Division of Distribution

Profit generated from sales of natural wealth shall be divided equally among the Commonwealth, the Satrapy containing the natural wealth, and the Shahrestan whose land the natural wealth comes from. Each shall receive one-third of the profits.

Article 8 Sovereignty Over Natural Wealth

(1) No government may force a Shahrestan to exploit the natural wealth within its borders.

(2) The Commonwealth shall not force a Satrapy to exploit the natural wealth within a Satrapy's borders.

Article 9 Limiting the Resource Curse
No government may use revenue from natural wealth to fund more than 15 percent of its budget per annum.

Article 10 Use of Food for Energy Production
(1) Agricultural land may not be used for the production of biofuel energy.
(2) Production of or the use of biofuels made from edible food products is prohibited in the Guarded Domains.

Section 3 Gold and Currency

Article 11 Gold Extraction
Gold extracted within the Guarded Domains's borders shall be sold to the Commonwealth at the global market value so that it may be turned into bullion for currency.

Article 12 Gold Standard[58]
(1) The Guarded Domains of Iranshahr shall have an economic system based on the gold bullion standard.
(2) All coin and banknotes issued by the Commonwealth must be backed one hundred percent by gold bullion.
(3) Gold coins issued by the Commonwealth or foreign gold coins of reliable purity may be used as mediums of exchange.
(4) The Commonwealth shall determine which foreign gold coins are acceptable for use in the Guarded Domains.

Article 13 Currency
(1) One troy ounce of gold is the equivalent of one Daric.
(2) One Daric is the equivalent of a hundred Dirhams.
(3) One Dirham is the equivalent ten Toman.
(4) One Toman is the equivalent of ten Rial.

Article 14 Silver as a Medium of Exchange

---

[58] Mark Skousen, *Economics of a Pure Gold Standard*, 3rd ed (Irvington-on-Hudson, N.Y: Foundation for Economic Education, 1996).

(1) Silver coinage may be used as a medium of exchange within the Guarded Domains.

(2) The relationship between the value of silver and gold shall be determined through a floating exchange rate.

(3) All tax revenue paid to the Commonwealth shall be in the form of gold darics or officially recognized international gold coins.

Section 4 Commonwealth Basics Examination

Article 15 Commonwealth Basics Examination Purpose

To ensure a common basis of knowledge for elected officials to the Commonwealth, all prospective officials must pass the Commonwealth Basics Examination.

Article 16 Structure of the Commonwealth Basics Examination

(1) The Commonwealth Basics Examination shall consist of multiple choice questions relating to topics with which political leaders should be acquainted.

(2) The exam shall consist of the following topics:

a. Content of the Commonwealth Constitution

b. Ethnicities of the Guarded Domains

c. Religions and Philosophies of the Guarded Domains

d. World Political Geography

Article 17 Creation of Commonwealth Basics Exam

The questions for the Commonwealth Basics Exam shall be created by randomly selecting questions from the Commonwealth Basics Book.

Article 18 Commonwealth Basics Book

(1) All questions in the Commonwealth Basics Examination shall be derived from information in the Commonwealth Basics Book.

(2) This book shall be made available for download on the internet free of charge or in printed edition at an affordable price.

(3) This book shall be written by a group of experts selected by their peers in the academic fields relevant to the book.

(4) The Commonwealth Basics Book shall consist of the following topic sections:

a. Content of the Commonwealth Constitution

b. Ethnicities of the Guarded Domains

c. Religions and Philosophies of the Guarded Domains

d. World Political Geography

(5) Each topic section shall have a questionnaire list consisting of questions that may be asked on the Commonwealth Basics Examination.

(6) Topic sections shall be peer reviewed for objectivity and relevance of information.

Section 5 Limits on Corrupt Behavior

Article 19 Aniconic Government

(1) Government funds shall not be used to create images of or monuments dedicated to a current member of government.

(2) Government funds shall not be used to create images of or monuments dedicated to a living former member of government.

(3) Political party funds shall not be used to create images of or monuments dedicated to party members unless it is during election season.

Article 20 Election Season

(1) A citizen seeking political office may declare their candidacy exactly one year away from the election day. They may start campaigning and start collecting campaign donations.

(2) A political candidate who campaigns or collects campaign donations prior to this date shall be required to pay a fine for the first violation and return the illicit donations.

(3) If a citizen violates this article a second time, they shall be barred from running for the office.

Article 21 Campaign Financing

(1) Political campaigns shall only be financed by donations from individuals domiciled in the Guarded Domains.

(2) A political candidate may receive financial contributions, goods, and services amounting to no more than one daric in value from an individual per election season.

Article 22 Justice Above All

(1) No member of government shall have immunity from prosecution.

(2) No member of government shall have the power to pardon criminal offenses.

Article 23 Transparent Finances

(1) No citizen shall hold accounts with any bank that does not disclose account information with the Satrapial, Enclave, or Commonwealth governments.

(2) No government official shall hold accounts with foreign banks.

(3) Money and precious commodities belonging to the Guarded Domains of Iranshahr shall not be stored outside of the country.

(4) Money and precious commodities belonging to the Guarded Domains of Iranshahr shall not be stored in private banks.

Article 24 Just Fees

(1) A fee shall be defined as a sum of money paid or charged for a service provided.

(2) Fees charged by a government must follow these criteria:

a. the fee price cannot exceed the government's cost to maintain the service.

b. the fee must be used for the maintenance of the service.

Article 25 Just Fines

(1) A fine shall be defined as a sum of money paid by an individual, business, or organization, which, by judgment of a competent jurisdiction, is required to be paid for the punishment of an offence.

(2) Government issued fines shall be charged as a percentage of an individual's, business's, or organization's annual income.

Article 26 Just Licenses, Permits, and Certifications

The costs of licenses, permits, or certifications shall not be so excessive that they create a profit for the issuer.

Article 27 Public Over Private Good

(1) Any business or individual that sells a good or service or uses a technology or business practice that can be directly linked to environmental degradation shall be held financially responsible for all damages related to the environmental degradation.

(2) Any business or individual that sells a good or service or uses a technology or business practice that can be directly linked to the harm of human health shall be held financially responsible for all damages related to the harm of human health.

(3) Any business or individual that sells a good or service or uses a technology or business practice that can be directly linked to harm of the Commonwealth economy shall be held financially responsible for all damages related to the Commonwealth economy.

Article 28 Usury

Any interest rate set above 15 percent per annum shall be considered usury and shall be prohibited within the Guarded Domains.

Article 29 Minimum Wage and Maximum Income

(1) An individual who works within the Guarded Domains cannot receive a total income of more than 250 darics per annum.

(2) Each Satrapy shall establish a minimum wage per hour of work.

(3) Each Satrapy may establish a maximum income under 250 darics per annum.

Article 30 Gross National Happiness[59]

The Commonwealth shall use the measure Gross National Happiness rather than Gross Domestic Product to inform its policies.

Article 31 Steady State Economy[60]

The Commonwealth shall work to shift Iranshahr's economy from a growth economy to a steady state economy.

Article 32 State Owned Banks

(1) All government funds shall be deposited in government owned banks.

(2) Government funds shall not be deposited in private banks.

Article 33 Just Expropriation

(1) In matters relating to expropriation, fair compensation shall be defined as paying the property owner 110 percent of the property's current market value at the time of acquisition.

(2) Expropriated properties cannot be sold or given to individuals or businesses.

(3) All expropriation deals shall be subject to public scrutiny and oversight.

(4) All governments shall be required to make an offer of purchase before using the powers of expropriation.

Article 34 Preventing Military Government

(1) Under no circumstances may members of the Defense Forces take political power.

(2) Under no circumstances may former members of the Defense Forces take political power within five years of leaving the Defense Forces.

(3) The Defense Forces shall not acquire sources of income independent of those allocated to it by the Commonwealth budget.

(4) The Defense Forces shall not be used to disperse protesters.

---

[59] UN. General Assembly (65th sess. : 2010–2011), "Happiness : Towards a Holistic Approach to Development :," August 25, 2011, http://digitallibrary.un.org/record/715187.

[60] Herman E Daly, *Beyond Growth: The Economics of Sustainable Environment* (Boston, Mass.: Beacon Press, 1996).

Article 35 Financial Conflicts of Interest

(1) Every public official, whether elected or appointed to a position of leadership, shall give the administration of their private business interests to an independent trust for the duration of their public service. They must also divest from all investment assets or business interests.

(2) Every public official, whether elected or appointed to a position of leadership, shall refrain from acquiring new investments or pursuing new private business interests during the duration of their time as a public official.

Article 36 Familial Conflicts of Interest

(1) Every public official, whether elected or appointed, shall refrain from hiring family members to positions under their jurisdiction.

(2) Family members include people related to the public official by blood relation or marriage ties. These include spouse, parents, children, grandparents, grandchildren, aunts, uncles, cousins, nieces, and nephews.

(3) Every public official, whether elected or appointed, shall refrain from hiring persons who have a romantic or sexual relationship with the public official.

Article 37 Preventing Hand Chosen Succession

(1) If an elected official leaves office before the end of their term, a special election shall be held four months from the day they step down.

(2) The newly elected official shall serve the duration of the term.

CHAPTER 4 TOPICS IN THE INTERNATIONAL SPHERE

Section 1 Foreign Aid

Article 1 Giving Aid

The Guarded Domains of Iranshahr may not give financial or military aid to nations or organizations that violate the Universal Declaration of Human Rights.

Article 2 Receiving Aid

Any aid to the Guarded Domains that limits its sovereignty must be approved by a majority of the People through a General Referendum.

Section 2 Rights for Enemy Combatants

Article 3 Purpose

The Guarded Domains of Iranshahr shall not punish the enemy soldier for their nation's transgressions. The Guarded Domains shall show captured enemy soldiers mercy and benevolence.

Article 4 Freedom from Abuse

Enemy combatants shall not be abused or tortured by anyone in the service of the Guarded Domains of Iranshahr.

Article 5 Right to Basic Necessities

Enemy combatants shall receive sufficient food, shelter, water, and healthcare while in captivity.

Section 3 Revaluation of International Arrangements

Article 6 Treaty Reevaluation

All treaties signed by illegitimate governments that have ruled Iranshahr before the Guarded Domains of Iranshahr was established shall be voted on by the People. A simple majority shall decide if a treaty is still favorable or unfavorable.

TITLE 5 RIGHTS, LIMITATIONS, AND DUTIES

CHAPTER 1 INDIVIDUAL RIGHTS, LIMITATIONS, AND DUTIES

Section 1 Individual Right

Article 1 The Individual
An individual shall be defined as a human being who is 18 years of age or older.

Article 2 Mastery of Self
(1) The individual is master of their mind, body, and spirit. Actions taken upon the self shall not be regulated or restricted by the government or another individual, so long as the action does not infringe on another individual's or child's rights.
(2) In the case of a pregnant individual or child, the fetus shall be considered a part of the individual's or child's body.

Article 3 Equality
(1) All human beings are equal before the law.
(2) No individual may be discriminated against by any government, citizen, individual, or business, namely for their origin, ethnicity, sex, age, sexual orientation,

language, class, religious, philosophical, or political beliefs, or because of a corporal, or mental disability.

(3) Women and men have equal rights. All levels of government shall provide for legal and factual equality, and shall endeavor to eliminate inequalities and inequities between women and men in all aspects of society. Women and men have the right to equal pay for work of equal value.

(4) The law provides for measures to eliminate barriers to and disadvantages of disabled people.

Article 4 Protection Against Arbitrary Actions

Every individual has the right to be treated by government institutions in good faith and without arbitrariness.

Article 5 Freedom from Inhumane Practices

(1) The death penalty shall be prohibited.

(2) Any form of cruel, inhumane, or degrading treatment or punishment shall be prohibited.

Article 6 Freedom from Harm

(1) Every individual shall be protected under the law against bodily, emotional, sexual, and mental harm.

(2) Every individual shall be protected under the law against verbal, physical, and sexual harassment.

Article 7 Right to Self-Defense

(1) Every individual shall have the right to use physical violence against another individual who directly attacks them with physical violence.

(2) Preemptive use of physical violence shall not be protected under this right.

Article 8 Right to Aid in Distress

Every individual in distress without the ability to take care of themselves has the right to assistance that can provide for a life led with human dignity.

Article 9 Protection of Privacy

(1) Every individual has the right to have their privacy respected.

(2) Every individual has the right over their personal data in all its forms.

(3) An individual's personal data cannot be given or sold to a third-party without their explicit permission.

(4) Every individual who has served a sentence for a non-violent crime has the right not to disclose their criminal past. An individual who has served a sentence for a violent crime can have their record expunged after a period of 10 years and have been found by a panel of experts to be reformed.

Article 10 Right to Sexuality

(1) Every individual shall have the right to give consent or refuse consent to engage in sexual activities with another individual or group of individuals.

(2) Consent shall be a positive affirmation to engage in sexual activities.

(3) Without positive affirmation of consent, the default assumption shall be refusal to give consent.

(4) Every individual shall have the right to refuse consent at any time during sexual activities.

(5) Every individual has the right to engage in sexual activities for payment.

Article 11 Right to Sexual & Reproductive Services

(1) Every individual has the right to procreate.

(2) Every individual has the right to use contraceptives.

(3) Every pregnant individual has the right to terminate a pregnancy at any time.

Article 12 Right to Substance Use

Every individual has the right to consume any substance at their own discretion.

Article 13 Freedom from Forced Labor

Forced labor shall be prohibited, regardless of whether the individual is free or imprisoned.

Article 14 Right to Die[61]

An individual has the right to die if the following steps are completed:

a. The individual makes a request for euthanasia to a licensed physician or psychologist voluntarily.

b. The individual completes three months of weekly one-hour therapy sessions with a licensed psychologist. A panel of three independent licensed psychologists will review documentation of the therapy sessions to ensure ethical standards have been followed.

---

[61] Judith A. C. Rietjens et al., "Two Decades of Research on Euthanasia from the Netherlands. What Have We Learnt and What Questions Remain?," *Journal of Bioethical Inquiry* 6, no. 3 (September 2009): 271–83, https://doi.org/10.1007/s11673-009-9172-3.

c.   The individual provides a written declaration of will to a judge stating their intention to die.

d.   The euthanasia is carried out by a physician or the individual, under the supervision of the physician, using a medically appropriate method.

Article 15 Right to Marriage, Domestic Partnership, and Family

(1) The definition of marriage shall not be defined by the government and therefore the idea of marriage shall be defined by the individuals seeking such a union.

(2) Every individual of age 18 years or older, without any limitation due to race, ethnicity, religion, class, gender, sexual orientation, or number of spouses, has the right to marry.

(3) Individuals shall enter into a marriage only with the free and full consent of the intending spouses.

(4) Spouses are entitled to equal rights within a marriage, during marriage and in divorce.

(5) Every married individual may at any time and for any reason, end a marriage with their spouse. The pronouncement of triple talaq is not a legal form of divorce.

(6) Every individual has the right to cohabitation with a partner or partners without entering into marriage, only with the free and full consent of the intending partners.

(7) Unmarried couples shall not be penalized by the state as compared to married couples.

(8) Every individual has the right to found a family.

(9) Every individual has the right to adopt a child, if they can be found to provide a safe and nurturing environment for the child and with the child's consent.

Article 16 Freedom of Religion, Philosophy, and Conscience[62]

(1) Every individual has the right to practice any religion, philosophy, or conscience they voluntarily choose.

(2) Every individual has the right to practice or profess their beliefs alone or in community with others.

(3) Every individual has the right to join or belong to a religious or philosophical community without coercion.

(4) Every individual has the right to receive religious or philosophical education without coercion.

(5) No individual may be punished for abandoning a religion or philosophy, or leaving a religious or philosophical community.

---

[62] United States and Fink, *The Constitution of the United States of America.*

(6) Every individual or group of individuals has the right to build a place of worship or congregation for their religion or philosophy.

Article 17 Freedom of Speech[63]
(1) Every individual has the right to form, express, and disseminate ideas through all means of direct and indirect communication.
(2) Every individual has the right to insult according to their desires.

Article 18 Freedom of Information
Every individual has the right to receive accurate information freely, to gather it from legally accessible sources, and to disseminate it.

Article 19 Freedom of the Media
(1) The freedom of the press, radio, television, internet, and all other forms of public broadcasting of productions and information is guaranteed.
(2) Censorship by government institutions or funded government organizations is prohibited.
(3) Individuals may submit pieces for public broadcasting under pseudonyms.
(4) Journalists have the right to keep their sources' personal information confidential. Subpoenas cannot be used to force a journalist to disclose their sources.

Article 20 Freedom of Language
Every individual has the right to speak, write, or read any language they desire.

Article 21 Right to Primary Education
Every individual has the right to empowering and free primary education.

Article 22 Freedom of Knowledge
Every individual has the right to pursue knowledge in all its forms.

Article 23 Freedom of Science
(1) The right to conduct scientific research shall be guaranteed.
(2) The teaching of accurate science shall be guaranteed.

Article 24 Freedom of Art
Every individual has the right to create and distribute art.

Article 25 Freedom of Assembly

---

[63] United States and Fink.

(1) Every individual has the right to assemble in the public sphere without a permit.

(2) Every individual has the right to organize assemblies, to participate in them, or to refrain from them.

Article 26 Freedom of Association

(1) Every individual has the right to associate with other individuals.

(2) Every individual has the right to form, to join, and to belong to associations.

(3) Every individual has the right to participate in association activities.

(4) No individual may be forced to join, to belong to, or to remain in an association.

Article 27 Protection Against Expulsion

(1) Refugees shall not be expelled from the Guarded Domains or extradited to a state in which they are persecuted.

(2) No individual may be extradited to a state where they are threatened by inhumane treatment or punishment.

Article 28 Right to Property

(1) Every individual has the right to own property.

(2) Expropriation or restrictions of ownership equivalent to expropriation shall be fairly compensated.

(3) No government shall acquire private property without the owner's consent and fair compensation given.

(4) The right to own real estate property does not extend to foreigners domiciled outside the Guarded Domains of Iranshahr.

Article 29 Economic Freedom

(1) Every individual has the right to pursue their economic ambitions.

(2) Every individual has the right to choose a profession or create a business.

Article 30 Right to Work

(1) Every individual has the right to work and shall not be prevented from finding employment.

(2) Every individual has the right to work under equitable and satisfactory conditions, and shall receive equal pay for equal work.

(3) Every individual shall not be forced to join a union or pay union dues and fees as a condition of employment.

Article 31 Right to Bankruptcy

Every individual has the right to bankruptcy proceedings if they cannot fulfill their liabilities.

Article 32 Freedom from Parental Debt[64]

(1) Debt acquired by an individual's parents or guardians shall not be passed on to the individual.

(2) Assets of the parents shall be used to pay debt. If debt exceeds asset value, the creditor shall take a loss.

Article 33 Protection of Contracts

(1) The individual shall have the right to create voluntary contracts with other individuals, groups of individuals, businesses, or other institutions.

(2) Contracts created voluntarily shall be protected under the law.

(3) Contracts created through coercion or under false pretenses shall be deemed invalid and compensation shall be awarded to the injured by the injurer.

(4) Contracts that contradict the Commonwealth Constitution or the Satrapial constitution of domicile shall be deemed invalid.

Article 34 General Procedural Guarantees

(1) In administrative and judicial proceedings, every individual has the right to equal and fair treatment.

(2) Every individual has the right to timely adjudication in administrative and judicial proceedings.

(3) All parties in a dispute have the right to be heard.

(4) Every individual has the right to free legal counsel.

Article 35 Guarantee of Legal Proceedings

Every individual has the right to have legal disputes arbitrated by judicial authority.

Article 36 Judicial Proceedings

(1) In cases to be decided in judicial proceedings, every individual has the right to an independent and impartial court with jurisdiction established by law. Exceptional tribunals are prohibited.

(2) For those involved in the civil action, every individual has the right to have the case adjudicated by the court of their domicile. The law may provide for another venue if impartiality or independence is threatened.

---

[64] Al Jazeera, "Bonded Labour : Spiraling Debt Trapping Pakistan's Brick Kiln Workers," accessed December 3, 2019, https://interactive.aljazeera.com/aje/2019/pakistan-bonded-labour/index.html.

(3) The parties involved in a civil action may choose a jury trial or a bench trial. Bench trials may consist of one judge or a panel of three judges.

(4) Court hearings and verdict pronouncements are public. The law may provide for exceptions if impartiality or independence is threatened.

Article 37 Habeas Corpus

(1) Every individual may only be deprived of their liberty in the manner prescribed by law.

(2) Every arrested individual has the right to be informed immediately of the reasons for their arrest and of their rights while in detainment. The individual must be informed in a language which they understand.

(3) Every arrested individual must have the opportunity to assert their rights.

(4) Every arrested individual has the right to have their close relatives informed.

(5) Every arrested individual has the right to an attorney. If the individual cannot afford to hire one, an attorney will be provided at the government's expense.

(6) Every individual accused of a nonviolent crime shall not be held in pretrial detention.

(7) Every individual taken into pretrial detention has the right to be brought before a judge within 24 hours of the arrest; the judge decides whether the individual remains in pretrial detention or is released.

(8) Every individual detained without a trial is entitled to petition a court at any time. The court decides on the lawfulness of the individual's detention as soon as possible.

(9) Every individual held in pretrial detention is entitled to a trial within one month of the time of confinement.

Article 38 Criminal Procedure

(1) Every individual accused of a crime shall be presumed innocent until sentenced according to law.

(2) Every individual accused of a crime has the right to be informed immediately and comprehensively of the charges against them. The accused individual must have the opportunity to assert their rights of defense.

Article 39 Right of Appeal

(1) Every individual, whether a plaintiff or defendant, has the right to appeal a verdict to a higher court.

(2) The appeal shall be reviewed by a panel of three randomly chosen judges of that higher court level. If the three judges unanimously support the lower court's verdict, then the verdict stands. If there is no unanimous decision or the decision contradicts the original verdict, another appeal to a higher court is allowed.

(3) There is no appeal process for a case adjudicated by the Commonwealth Court, as it is the highest court in the Guarded Domains.

Article 40 Compensation for Wrongful Confinement
(1) Every imprisoned individual who is found innocent of the charges against them shall be compensated one daric per week of confinement.
(2) Every imprisoned individual who was charged with crime and is later found innocent shall be compensated two darics per week of confinement.

Article 41 Right to Restorative Justice
Every individual convicted of a crime has the right to restorative justice if the victim(s) of the crime consent(s) to its implementation.

Article 42 Right of Petition
(1) Every individual has the right to petition the government officials in their Shahrestan, Satrapy, and at the Commonwealth level; no disadvantages may arise from using this right.
(2) The authorities have to take cognizance of petitions.

Article 43 Statutes of Limitations
Every individual has the right to obtain justice. Statutes of limitations shall be prohibited.

Section 2 Individual Limitations

Article 44 Immigrant Individuals and Real Estate
Every individual who immigrates to the Guarded Domains shall reside within the Guarded Domains for 24 months before they shall have the right to purchase real estate.

Article 45 Limits on Substance Use
(1) No individual shall use alcohol, tobacco, or drugs in public spaces.
(2) No individual may operate machines of any kind while intoxicated with alcohol or drugs.

Article 46 Interlocking Directorates[65]
No individual shall serve on the board of more than one corporate business.

Article 47 Diplomatic Immunity
All foreign individuals presiding within the Guarded Domains's borders are subject to its laws. Diplomatic immunity shall be prohibited.

Article 48 Lobbying and Political Donations
(1) No individual shall compensate another individual or organization to attempt to influence government action through either oral or written communication on their behalf. Compensation includes money, gifts, or free or discounted services.
(2) No individual shall solicit compensation for attempting to influence government action.
(3) No individual shall receive money, gifts, or services from another individual or organization and donate it to a political candidate or political initiative on their behalf.

Article 49 Sharing Other People's Content
No individual may share content that identifies another individual without that individual's explicit consent. This content includes videos, physical or digital images, and voice recordings.

Section 3 Individual Compulsory Duties[66]

Article 50 Duty to Pay Taxes
Every individual has the duty to pay their legal share of taxes.

Article 51 Duty to Citizen's Service
Every individual seeking citizenship in the Guarded Domains of Iranshahr must attend Citizen's Service.

Article 52 Duty to Laws
(1) Every individual has the duty to obey the laws of the Commonwealth, the Satrapy of domicile, and the Shahrestan of domicile.

---

[65] Louis Dembitz Brandeis and Melvin I. Urofsky, *Other People's Money and How the Bankers Use It*, The Bedford Series in History and Culture (Boston: Bedford Books of St. Martin's Press, 1995).
[66] David Selbourne, *The Principle of Duty: An Essay on the Foundations of the Civic Order* (Notre Dame, Ind: University of Notre Dame Press, 2001).

(2) Every individual has the duty to report all violations of the Constitution or the law, regardless if the violation is against them or against another individual.

Article 53 Duty to Family
Every individual has the duty to protect their family members from physical, sexual, emotional, and mental harm.

Article 54 Duty to Children
(1) Every individual who has a child, either through their progeny or through legal adoption, has the duty to raise that child. In the event that both parents give the child up for adoption, both parents forfeit their parental rights and duties over the child.

(2) Every individual has the duty to register the birth of their child with the government of the Satrapy in which the birth occurred.

(3) Every individual has the duty to have their child vaccinated for all legally required vaccinations.

(4) Every individual has the duty to provide their child emotional and financial support until the child has reached the age of 18 years.

(5) Every individual has the duty to protect their child from physical, sexual, emotional, and mental harm.

(6) Every individual has the duty to keep their child in school until that child has reached the age of 18 years.

(7) Every individual has the duty to disallow their child from marrying and shall refrain from marrying their child to another child or individual until that child reaches the age of 18 years.

Article 55 Duty to the Stranger
(1) Every individual has the duty to help any stranger who calls for aid.

(2) In the event a stranger is unconscious or otherwise unable to call for aid, every individual has constitutional protection from legal repercussions if they aid the stranger.

Article 56 Duty to the Contract
Every individual has the duty to uphold their obligations in a contract created voluntarily.

Article 57 Duty to Decency
Every individual has the duty to treat other individuals as equals, regardless of gender, race, ethnicity, religion, sexual orientation, political affiliation, or economic status.

Article 58 Duty to Reciprocity
Every individual has the duty to not act with other individuals in a manner that they would not want other individuals to act with them.

Article 59 Duty to Preventative Health
(1) Every individual has the duty to receive all preventative health services and procedures recommended by the Commonwealth Health Insurance Company, and to receive these preventative health services and procedures during the recommended time period.
(2) Every individual has the duty to prevent the spread of disease by their actions.

Article 60 Duty to Animals
Every individual has the duty to not cause any animal harm unless that harm is lethal and with the purpose of preparing that animal for human consumption.

Article 61 Duty to Cleanliness
(1) Every individual has the duty to keep their domicile or property clean of waste that could create foul odors, habitat for pests, or dangers to human or environmental health.
(2) Every individual has the duty to dispose any type of waste in designated receptacles or official landfills.
(3) Every individual has the duty to pick up litter in public spaces.

Article 62 Duty to Aid the Law
Every individual has the duty to aid a peace officer who requires their assistance in apprehending a suspect or protecting the law.

Article 63 Duty to Provide Testimony
Every individual has the duty to provide testimony if subpoenaed by a court of law.

Article 64 Duty to Truth
Every individual has the duty to bare true testament under oath.

Article 65 Duty to the Census
Every individual has the duty to participate in the decennial census.

Section 4 Individual Noncompulsory Duties

Article 66 Duty to Seek Aid

Every individual has the duty to ask for help of other individuals when they are in need of aid.

Article 67 Duty to Moderation[67]
(1) Every individual has the duty to moderate their speech, thoughts, actions, and desires.
(2) Every individual has the duty to refrain from accumulating resources beyond their need.

Article 68 Duty to Procreation
(1) Every individual has the duty to limit the number of children they beget to two children.
(2) Every individual has the duty to wait to procreate until they have the financial, emotional, and mental capacity to provide a child with a high quality of life.

Article 69 Duty to Tradition
(1) Every individual has the duty to promote and protect traditions or customs that enhance the quality of life of the individual and create solidarity between individuals.
(2) Every individual has the duty to abandon traditions or customs that are harmful to the individual's quality of life or maintain inequality or inequity between individuals.

Article 70 Duty to Parents
Every individual has the duty to provide care for their elderly parents if; their parents are financially, physically, or mentally incapable of living independently, and their parents satisfied their parental duties to their child.

Article 71 Duty to Health
(1) Every individual has the duty to maintain their physical, emotional, and mental health.
(2) Every individual has the duty to refrain from using drugs that cause health risks.
(3) Every individual has the duty to refrain from smoking.
(4) Every individual has the duty to eat a healthy diet.
(5) Every individual has the duty to exercise regularly.
(6) Every individual has the duty to use counseling services regularly.

---

[67] Aristotle, *Ethics: The Nichomachean Ethics* (Baltimore: Penguin Books, 1966).

Article 72 Duty to Charity
Every individual has the duty to give a portion of their income to charity.

Article 73 Duty to Volunteer
Every individual has the duty to give a portion of their time and skills in voluntary service to the community.

CHAPTER 2 CITIZENSHIP & CITIZEN RIGHTS, LIMITATIONS, AND DUTIES

Section 1 Citizenship

Article 1 Citizenship
Every individual, upon graduating primary education and taking the Citizen's Service, shall be granted citizenship and access to all the political rights citizenship entails.

Article 2 Acquisition and Loss of Citizenship
(1) The Commonwealth regulates the acquisition and the loss of citizenship.
(2) Every citizen imprisoned shall forfeit their political rights for the duration of imprisonment.

Article 3 Exercise of Political Rights
(1) The Commonwealth regulates the exercise of political rights in Commonwealth matters; the Satrapies regulate the exercise of these rights in Satrapial and Shahrestan matters.
(2) Political rights are exercised at the place of domicile.
(3) The Satrapies may provide that new resident citizens exercise their political rights in Satrapial and Shahrestan matters only after a waiting period of up to three months following their taking of residence.

Section 2 Citizen Rights

Article 4 Right to Vote

(1) Every citizen has the right to vote in relevant elections and referendums of the Commonwealth.

(2) Every citizen has the right to vote in relevant elections and referendums in the Satrapy of their domicile.

(3) Every citizen has the right to vote in relevant elections and referendums in the Shahrestan of their domicile.

Article 5 Right to Petition

Every citizen has the right to petition their elected officials.

Article 6 Right to Peaceful Protest

Every citizen has the right to protest peacefully in public spaces.

Article 7 Right to Loiter

Every citizen has the right to loiter in public spaces.

Article 8 Freedom of Domicile and Movement

(1) Every citizen has the right to establish domicile anywhere within the Guarded Domains.

(2) They have the right to leave or to return to Guarded Domains.

(3) No citizen may be expelled from the country; they may be extradited to a foreign authority only with their consent.

Article 9 Citizens Domiciled Abroad

Citizens domiciled outside of the Guarded Domains shall have access to the same rights, limitations, and duties of citizens domiciled within the Guarded Domains, in particular regarding the exercise of political rights at the commonwealth level.

Article 10 Basic Income[68]

(1) Every citizen shall receive a sum granted by the Satrapy of domicile for basic human needs.

(2) Basic human needs shall be defined as food, water, and shelter.

(3) Basic income shall be granted in monthly installments.

(4) Every citizen serving prison sentences shall not receive basic income for the duration of incarceration.

(5) Basic income shall replace all other forms of welfare.

(6) All other forms of government welfare are prohibited.

---

[68] Ravents, *Against Charity.*

Article 11 Right to a Passport
Every citizen has the right to acquire a passport.

Article 12 Right to Own Firearms
Every citizen has the right to own one or more firearms after the completion of the following proceedings:

(1) The citizen shall take and pass a gun safety class, and shall take and pass a gun safety class every two years.

(2) The citizen shall have a background check before receiving the firearm.

(3) The citizen shall pass a psychological review with a licensed psychologist.

(3) The citizen shall register the firearm with the Satrapy of domicile.

Article 13 Right to Form a Militia
(1) Every citizen has the right to form or join a militia.

(2) Every militia and its members must be registered with the Satrapy of domicile and with the Commonwealth.

(3) Every militia shall act as support in times of war and natural disasters.

(4) No militia shall act as law enforcement without Satrapial approval and training in times of war and natural disaster.

(5) The number of members per militia shall be restricted to one thousand members.

Article 14 Right to Serve
(1) Every citizen of qualifying physical and mental health has the right to serve in the Savaran, the Navy, the Air Force, the Commonwealth Militia, and the Nonviolent Defense Force.

(2) The Commonwealth and the Armed Forces reserve the right to limit the size of the armed forces.

Article 15 Freedom from Drafts
(1) No government shall issue a draft for the citizens of the Guarded Domains of Iranshahr.

(2) All military service shall be voluntary.

Article 16 Right to Participate in Government
(1) Every citizen has the right to propose legislation to a General Referendum or a Satrapial Referendum.

(2) Every citizen has the right serve in government.

Article 17 Right to Run for Political Office
(1) Every citizen over the age of 18 and under the age of 75 has the right to run for political office in the Commonwealth government.
(2) Every citizen over the age of 18 and under the age limit set by their Satrapy of domicile has the right to run for political office in their Satrapy of domicile.

Section 3 Citizen Limitations

Article 18 Geographical Limits on Exercise of Political Rights
(1) No citizen may exercise political rights in more than one Satrapy.
(2) No citizen may exercise political rights in more than one Shahrestan.

Article 19 Selling of Votes
No citizen may sell their votes, or purchase another citizen's votes.

Section 4 Citizen Compulsory Duties

Article 20 Duty to Registration
Every citizen has the duty to register for voting in their domicile. Failure to register may result in a fine decided by the Satrapies.

Article 21 Duty to Jury Participation
(1) Every citizen has the duty to participate in jury of the Shahrestan they are domiciled if they are chosen by lottery.
(2) No citizen shall participate in a jury more than once per year.

Article 22 Guardians of Justice
Every citizen has the duty to challenge unfair practices or laws through legal, civil, and nonviolent means.

Section 5 Citizen Noncompulsory Duties

Article 23 Duty to Elected Office
The citizen has the duty to seek elected office at least once in their adult life.

Article 24 Duty to Open-Mindedness
The citizen has the duty to learn about perspectives different from their own.

CHAPTER 3 CHILDREN'S RIGHTS, LIMITATIONS, AND DUTIES

Section 1 Child Rights

Article 1 Definition of Child
A child shall be defined as any human below the age of 18. A fetus shall not be considered a child.

Article 2 Basic Income
Every child has the right to a basic income that satisfies their need for food, water, and shelter.

Article 3 Education
Every child has the right to free primary education.

Article 4 Right to Protection
Every child has the right to protection from neglect, exploitation, abuse, and discrimination.

Article 5 Custody
In matters of child custody, the judiciary shall decide which parent or guardian is better suited as custodian. Each parent shall be analyzed for mental health, financial security, and history of abuse to determine custody.

Article 6 Right to Health Care
Every child has the right to adequate health care.

Article 7 Freedom from Genital Mutilation
No child shall receive modifications to their genitalia that shall cause pain during sexual intercourse in adulthood.

Article 8 Child Passport
Every child has the right to acquire a passport.

Section 2 Child Limitations

Article 9 Consent

No child may consent to the following:

(1) Engaging in a sexual relationship with another child or individual.

(2) Engaging in a marriage with another child or individual.

(3) Engaging in any contract with another child or individual.

Article 10 Work Restrictions

(1) No child under sixteen years of age may engage in work.

(2) Children that can work may only work for a total of twenty hours per week.

Section 3 Child Compulsory Duties

Article 11 Duty to Attend School

(1) Every child has the duty to attend school until they graduate from primary school.

(2) Every child has the duty to be present in school on every class day for the full duration of the class schedule.

Article 12 Duty to Avoid Drugs, Alcohol, and Smoking

Every child has the duty to avoid using drugs, alcohol, or any tobacco products.

CHAPTER 4 BUSINESS RIGHTS, LIMITATIONS AND DUTIES

Article 1 Business Definition

A business shall be defined as an organization or entity engaged in commercial, industrial, or professional activities.

Article 2 Business Organization Definitions

(1) A sole proprietorship shall be defined as an unincorporated business with a single owner who pays personal income tax on profits earned from the business.

(2) A partnership shall be defined as a business in which two or more individuals share the profits and liabilities.

(3) A corporation shall be defined as a legal entity that is separate and distinct from its owners.

(4) A limited liability company shall be defined as corporate business whereby the members of the company cannot be held personally liable for the company's debts or liabilities.

(5) A cooperative shall be defined as a business owned and democratically controlled by individuals who produce or consume the business's goods or services, or are the business's employees.

Section 1 Business Rights

Article 3 Protection of Business Contracts
(1) Every business shall have the right to create voluntary contracts with other individuals, groups of individuals, businesses, or other institutions.

(2) Contracts created voluntarily shall be protected under the law.

(3) Contracts created through coercion or under false pretenses shall be deemed invalid and compensation shall be awarded to the injured by the injurer.

(4) Contracts that contradict the Commonwealth Constitution or the Satrapial constitution of domicile shall be deemed invalid.

Article 4 Protection of Business Property
(1) Every business has the right to own property.

(2) Expropriation and restrictions of ownership equivalent to expropriation are fairly compensated.

(3) No government shall acquire a business' property without the business owner or owners' consent and fair compensation given.

(4) The right to own real estate property does not extend to foreign businesses domiciled outside the Guarded Domains of Iranshahr.

Article 5 Right to Advertise
Every business has the right to advertise its goods or services.

Article 6 General Procedural Guarantees
(1) In administrative and judicial proceedings, every business has the right to equal and fair treatment.

(2) Every business has the right to timely adjudication in administrative and judicial proceedings.

(3) All parties in a dispute have the right to be heard.

(4) Every business has the right to free legal counsel.

Article 7 Guarantee of Legal Proceedings
Every business has the right to have legal disputes arbitrated by judicial authority.

Article 8 Judicial Proceedings
(1) In cases to be decided in judicial proceedings, every business has the right to an independent and impartial court with jurisdiction established by law. Exceptional tribunals are prohibited.

(2) For those involved in the civil action, every business has the right to have the case adjudicated by the court of its domicile. The law may provide for another venue if impartiality or independence is threatened.

(3) Court hearings and verdict pronouncements are public. The law may provide for exceptions if impartiality or independence is threatened.

Article 9 Criminal procedure
(1) Every business accused of a crime shall be presumed innocent until sentenced according to law.

(2) Every business accused of a crime has the right to be informed immediately and comprehensively of the charges against it. The accused business must have the opportunity to assert its rights of defense.

Article 10 Right of Petition
(1) Every business has the right to petition the government officials in its Shahrestan, Satrapy, and at the Commonwealth level; no disadvantages may arise from using this right.

(2) The authorities must take cognizance of petitions.

Article 11 Right to Bankruptcy
Every business has the right to bankruptcy proceedings.

Section 2 Business Limitations

Article 12 Non-personhood
(1) Businesses shall not be equated as individuals.
(2) Businesses shall not be equated as citizens.

Article 13 Corporate Liability
(1) Corporate liability shall not extend to criminal laws.
(2) Individuals who direct a business to conduct illegal activities shall be responsible for their own actions.

(3) Responsibility for crimes committed through a business shall reside with the business's leadership during the time in which the crime took place, unless a specific individual or group of individuals can be proven guilty of the actions leading to the business committing the crime.

Article 14 Separation of Business and State
(1) Businesses are prohibited from proposing or writing legislation.

(2) Businesses are prohibited from funding political campaigns of any kind.

(3) Businesses are prohibited from advising politicians on legislation, regulation, or law.

Article 15 Not-For-Profit Corporate Bodies
The following fee-for-service corporate bodies shall be designated as not-for-profit private businesses:

a. Educational institutions

b. Insurance providers

c. Hospitals

d. Pharmaceutical drug manufacturers

e. Arms producers

f. News media

Article 16 Price Gouging
In the event of a disaster, either natural or human made, no business shall raise the prices of goods or services more than 10 percent for the duration of the disaster.

Article 17 Truthful Advertising
No business shall engage in the following advertisement practices:

(1) Using visual aids besides the image of the product or service in an advertisement.

(2) Paying to place products in entertainment pieces.

(3) Making claims without citing evidence source.

Article 18 Anti-Competition
(1) No Business shall engage in any contract that reduces competition. These shall include:

a. Market allocation

b. Bid rigging

c. Price fixing

d. Monopolies

e. Oligopolies

Section 4 Business Compulsory Duties

Article 19 Duty to Pay Corporate Taxes
Every business has the duty to pay its legal share in taxes.

Article 20 Duty to Salary Transparency
Every business, whether publicly owned or privately owned, shall make available to the public all employee salaries or wages.

Article 21 International Policy
(1) Every business that has domicile within the Guarded Domains shall implement the corporate limitations while doing business in other countries.
(2) Every business shall treat individuals employed in other countries with the same rights that this document provides the People of Iranshahr.

CHAPTER 5 EMPLOYER RIGHTS, LIMITATIONS, AND DUTIES

Section 1 Employer Rights

Article 1 Right to Fire
Every employer has the right to fire an employee who does not meet the requirements of the contract agreed upon between employer and employee.

Article 2 Right to Layoff
After salaries of management are reduced by 25 percent for the next 12 months, every employer has the right to lay off more than five percent of employees during the fiscal year.

Article 3 Right to Ask
Every employer has the right to ask an employee to work on weekends, holidays, or more than forty hours a week. An employer has the right to encourage employees to work more with bonuses or overtime pay.

Article 4 Right to Lockout

Every employer has the right to lockout, provided it concerns labor relations and does not violate any obligation to keep labor peace or to resort to conciliation.

Section 2 Employer Limitations

Article 5 Protection of Off-Hours

No employer shall contact employees during off-hours. Exceptions will be made for emergencies that are documented.

Article 6 Government Documents

No employer shall hold an employee's government issued documents.

Article 7 Non-Specified Tasks

No employer shall threaten an employee with firing if an employee refuses to complete a task that is not specified in the contract between the employer and employee.

Article 8 Confidentiality Agreement

No employer may create confidentiality agreements with an employee if such a contract prevents that employee from disclosing illegal activity done by the employer or another employee.

Article 9 Past Crimes

(1) No employer may ask a job applicant if they have been convicted of a crime.

(2) No employer may conduct or request a criminal background check of a job applicant.

(3) Exceptions are made for job positions that work with children.

Section 3 Employer Compulsory Duties

Article 10 Duty to Contractual Work

Every employer has the duty to create a contract with their or its employee specifying all tasks, payments, and benefits. This shall be made before the individual is hired as an employee.

Article 11 Duty to Proper Compensation

(1) Every employer has the duty to compensate an employee the full amount in wages or salary agreed upon by contract between the employer and employee.

(2) Every employer has the duty to compensate an employee at time intervals agreed upon by contract between the employer and employee.

(3) If the employer is late in paying an employee, the employer shall pay the employee compounded interest on the arrears due to the employee. The compounded interest for arrears shall be set to a minimum annual rate of seven percent.

Article 12 Duty to Eliminate Workplace Sexual Harassment
Every employer has the duty to fire employees who sexually harass coworkers or subordinates.

Article 13 Duty to Workplace Health
(1) Every employer has the duty to keep their or its workplace hygienic.
(2) Every employer has the duty to send an employee home if they are ill.

CHAPTER 6 EMPLOYEE RIGHTS, LIMITATIONS, AND DUTIES

Section 1 Employee Rights

Article 1 Employee Definition
Every employee shall be defined as an individual who works for another individual or corporate body.

Article 2 Right to Weekend
Every employee has the right to two weekend days of their own choosing per week.

Article 3 Right to Paid Leave
Every employee has the right to a minimum of 10 paid leave days per year.

Article 4 Right to Paid Sick Leave
Every employee has the right to a minimum of five paid sick days per year.

Article 5 Right to Refuse Un-Negotiated Tasks

Every employee has the right to refuse to do tasks deemed unsafe by the employee or which are not explicitly stated in the contract between employee and employer.

Article 6 Right to Maternity or Paternity Leave

(1) Every employee has the right to three months paid leave if they have recently given birth to or adopted a newborn child.

(2) Every employee has the right to return to their job after maternity or paternity leave.

Article 7 Right to Refuse Overtime Work

Every employee has the right to refuse working on holidays, weekends, or more than forty hours per week without threat of punishment or expulsion from employment.

Article 8 Right to Report Employer Illegal Activity

(1) Every employee has the right to report employer misdeeds to law enforcement. The employee cannot be fired, sued, or charged for crimes for whistle blowing

(2) This right extends to employees of governments.

Article 9 Right to Unionize

(1) Every employee with their coworkers has the right to protect their interests.

(2) Every employee with their coworkers has the right to form unions, to join existing unions, or to refrain from joining unions.

(3) Conflicts between employees and employers should to be settled by negotiation and mediation when possible.

(4) A union has the right to strike, provided it concerns labor relations and does not violate any obligation to keep labor peace or to resort to conciliation.

Section 2 Employee Limitations

Article 10 Tenure

No employee may force their employer to grant them tenure.

Section 3 Employee Compulsory Duties

Article 11 Duty to the Contract

Every employee has the duty to fulfill their contractual obligations.

Latif Simorghi
KVIMOTEFINALLATINO
06/10/2019

Bibliography

Aristotle. *Ethics: The Nichomachean Ethics.* Baltimore: Penguin Books, 1966.

Asgharzadeh, Alireza. *Iran and the Challenge of Diversity: Islamic Fundamentalism, Aryanist Racism, and Democratic Struggles.* 1st ed. New York: Palgrave Macmillan, 2007.

Babayan, Kathryn. *Mystics, Monarchs, and Messiahs: Cultural Landscapes of Early Modern Iran.* Harvard Middle Eastern Monographs 35. Cambridge, Mass: Distributed for the Center for Middle Eastern Studies of Harvard University by Harvard University Press, 2002.

Bartol' d, V. V., and Clifford Edmund Bosworth. *An Historical Geography of Iran.* Modern Classics in Near Eastern Studies. Princeton, N.J: Princeton University Press, 1984.

Bingle, Benjamin. "A Matter of Size: Examining Representation and Responsiveness in State Legislatures and City Councils." Ph.D., Northern Illinois University, 2016. http://search.proquest.com/docview/1795559337/abstract/37C57A51C9BA42 EDPQ/1.

Boroujerdi, Mehrzad, ed. *Mirror for the Muslim Prince: Islam and the Theory of Statecraft.* First edition. Modern Intellectual and Political History of the Middle East. Syracuse, New York: Syracuse University Press, 2013.

Brandeis, Louis Dembitz, and Melvin I. Urofsky. *Other People's Money and How the Bankers Use It.* The Bedford Series in History and Culture. Boston: Bedford Books of St. Martin's Press, 1995.

Brown, Wendy. *Undoing the Demos: Neoliberalism's Stealth Revolution.* New York: Zone Books, 2017.

Bulliet, Richard W. *The Patricians of Nishapur: A Study in Medieval Islamic Social History.* Cambridge: Harvard University Press, 2008.

Koerdisch Instituut Brussel. "Charter of the Social Contract in Rojava (Syria)," February 7, 2014. https://www.kurdishinstitute.be/en/charter-of-the-social-contract/.

Chua, Amy. *Day of Empire: How Hyperpowers Rise to Global Dominance and Why They Fall.* New York, N.Y.: Anchor Books, 2009.

Church, Clive H., and Randolph Conrad Head. *A Concise History of Switzerland.* Cambridge Concise Histories. Cambridge: Cambridge University Press, 2013.

Dagger, Richard. *Civic Virtues: Rights, Citizenship, and Republican Liberalism.* Oxford Political Theory. New York: Oxford University Press, 1997.

Daly, Herman E. *Beyond Growth: The Economics of Sustainable Environment.* Boston, Mass.: Beacon Press, 1996.

Daryaee, Touraj. *Šahrestānīhā-ī Ērānšahr: a Middle Persian text on late antique geography, epic, and history : with English and Persian translations*. Costa Mesa, Calif.: Mazda Publishers, 2002.

Diamond, Jared M. *Guns, Germs, and Steel: The Fates of Human Societies*. New York: Norton, 2005.

Farmanfarmaian, Roxane. *War and Peace in Qajar Persia: Implications Past and Present*. History and Society in the Islamic World. New York: Routledge, 2015.

Farrokh, Kaveh. *Iran at War, 1500-1988*. Oxford ; Long Island City, NY: Osprey Publishing, 2011.

———. *The Armies of Ancient Persia: The Sassanians*, 2017.

Fisman, Raymond, and Miriam A. Golden. *Corruption: What Everyone Needs to Know*. What Everyone Needs to Know. New York: Oxford University Press, 2017.

Forsyth, Murray Greensmith. *Unions of States: The Theory and Practice of Confederation*. New York: Leicester University Press : Holmes & Meier, 1981.

Freire, Paulo, Donaldo P. Macedo, and Ira Shor. *Pedagogy of the Oppressed*. Translated by Myra Bergman Ramos. 50th anniversary edition. New York: Bloomsbury Academic, 2018.

Frost, Robert I. *The Oxford History of Poland-Lithuania: Volume 1: The Making of the Polish-Lithuanian Union, 1385-1569*, 2018.

Galeano, Eduardo Hughes. *Open Veins of Latin America (Las Venas Abiertas de América Latina, Engl.). Five Centuries of the Pillage of a Continent*. New York: Monthly Review Press, 1973.

Hamilton, Alexander, James Madison, John Jay, and Richard R. Beeman, eds. *The Federalist Papers*. Civic Classics 3. New York: Penguin Books, 2012.

Harris, Colette. *Control and Subversion: Gender Relations in Tajikistan*. London: Pluto Press, 2004.

Hodgson, Marshall G. S. *The Classical Age of Islam*. His The Venture of Islam ; v. 1. Chicago: University of Chicago Press, 1974.

———. *The Expansion of Islam in the Middle Periods*. His The Venture of Islam ; v. 2. Chicago: University of Chicago Press, 1974.

hooks, bell. *The Will to Change: Men, Masculinity, and Love*. 1st Atria Books hardcover ed. New York: Atria Books, 2004.

Hopkirk, Peter. *The Great Game: The Struggle for Empire in Central Asia*. New York: Kodansha International, 1992.

ʻAṭṭār, Farīd al-Dīn, Dick Davis, and Afkham Darbandi. *The Conference of the Birds*. The Penguin Classics. Harmondsworth, Middlesex, England ; New York, N.Y., U.S.A: Penguin Books, 1984.

Ibn Khaldūn, and Franz Rosenthal. *The Muqaddimah: An Introduction to History*. Princeton, N.J: Princeton University Press, 1980.

Jazeera, Al. "Bonded Labour : Spiraling Debt Trapping Pakistan's Brick Kiln Workers." Accessed December 3, 2019. https://interactive.aljazeera.com/aje/2019/pakistan-bonded-labour/index.html.

Jefferson, Thomas, and Barbara Oberg. *The Papers of Thomas Jefferson*. Princeton, N.J.; Woodstock: Princeton University Press, 2008.

Kasser, Tim. *The High Price of Materialism*. Cambridge, Mass: MIT Press, 2002.

Kuran, Timur. *The Long Divergence: How Islamic Law Held Back the Middle East*. Princeton; Oxford: Princeton University Press, 2013.

Lister, Frederick K. *The Early Security Confederations: From the Ancient Greeks to the United Colonies of New England*. Contributions in Political Science, Global Perspectives in History and Politics, no. 388. Westport, Conn: Greenwood Press, 1999.

Machiavelli, Niccolò, Bernard Crick, Leslie J Walker, and Brian Richardson. *The Discourses [of] Niccolò Machiavelli*. Harmondsworth: Penguin, 1970.

Manz, Beatrice Forbes. *The Rise and Rule of Tamerlane*. Cambridge Studies in Islamic Civilization. Cambridge ; New York: Cambridge University Press, 1989.

McCormick, John P. *Machiavellian Democracy*. Cambridge, [England] ; New York: Cambridge University Press, 2011.

Meisami, Julie Scott. *The Sea of Precious Virtues*. University of Utah Press, 1991.

Michael Knapp, Anja Flach, and Ercan Ayboga. *Revolution in Rojava Democratic Autonomy and Women's Liberation in Syrian Kurdistan*. Pluto Press, 2016.

Öcalan, Abdullah. *Democratic Confederalism*, 2014.

Perry, John R. *Karīm Khān Zand: A History of Iran, 1747-1779*. Publications of the Center for Middle Eastern Studies ; No. 12. Chicago: University of Chicago Press, 1979.

Pettit, Philip. *Republicanism: A Theory of Freedom and Government*. Oxford Political Theory. Oxford : New York: Clarendon Press ; Oxford University Press, 1997.

Plato, and Desmond Lee. *Plato: The Republic*. London: Penguin, 2003.

Pourshariati, Parvaneh. *Decline and Fall of the Sasanian Empire: The Sasanian-Parthian Confederacy and the Arab Conquest of Iran*. London ; New York : New York: I.B. Tauris in association with the Iran Heritage Foundation ; Distributed in the U.S.A. by Palgrave Macmillan, 2008.

Proudhon, P.-J., and Richard Vernon. *The Principle of Federation*. Toronto ; Buffalo: University of Toronto Press, 1979.

Ravents, Daniel/ Wark, Julie. *Against Charity*. Consortium Book Sales & Dist, 2018.

Reid, T. R. *The Healing of America: A Global Quest for Better, Cheaper, and Fairer Health Care : [With an Explenation of the 2010 Health Reform Bill*. New York: Penguin Books, 2010.

Rietjens, Judith A. C., Paul J. van der Maas, Bregje D. Onwuteaka-Philipsen, Johannes J. M. van Delden, and Agnes van der Heide. "Two Decades of Research on Euthanasia from the Netherlands. What Have We Learnt and What Questions Remain?" *Journal of Bioethical Inquiry* 6, no. 3 (September 2009): 271–83. https://doi.org/10.1007/s11673-009-9172-3.

Rousseau, Jean-Jacques. *The Social Contract.* Penguin Books Great Ideas. New York: Penguin Books, 2006.

Selbourne, David. *The Principle of Duty: An Essay on the Foundations of the Civic Order.* Notre Dame, Ind: University of Notre Dame Press, 2001.

Shahbazi, A. Shapur. "CROWN Iv. Persian Rulers from Arab Conquerors." In *Encyclopaedia Iranica*, V1:421–25. Accessed December 5, 2019. http://www.iranicaonline.org/articles/crown-iv.

Skousen, Mark. *Economics of a Pure Gold Standard.* 3rd ed. Irvington-on-Hudson, N.Y: Foundation for Economic Education, 1996.

Soudavar, Abolala. *The Aura of Kings: Legitimacy and Divine Sanction in Iranian Kingship.* Bibliotheca Iranica, no. 10. Costa Mesa, Calif: Mazda Publishers, 2003.

Starr, S. Frederick. *Lost Enlightenment: Central Asia's Golden Age from the Arab Conquest to Tamerlane.* Princeton University Press, 2015. https://press.princeton.edu/books/paperback/9780691165851/lost-enlightenment.

Steinberg, Jonathan. *Why Switzerland?* Cambridge: Cambridge Univ. Press, 1996.

Switzerland. *Federal Constitution of the Swiss Confederation of 18 April 1999: (Status as of 27 September 2009).,* 2009.

Thornton, Mark, and Marc Ulrich. "Constituency Size and Government Spending." *Public Finance Review* 27, no. 6 (November 1, 1999): 588–98. https://doi.org/10.1177/109114219902700602.

Tromborg, Mathias Wessel, and Leslie A. Schwindt- Bayer. "Constituent Demand and District-Focused Legislative Representation." *Legislative Studies Quarterly* 44, no. 1 (2019): 35–64. https://doi.org/10.1111/lsq.12217.

UN. General Assembly (65th sess. : 2010-2011). "Happiness : Towards a Holistic Approach to Development :," August 25, 2011. http://digitallibrary.un.org/record/715187.

United States, and Sam Fink, eds. *The Constitution of the United States of America: To Honor the Two-Hundredth Anniversary, September 17, 1987.* 1st ed. New York: Random House, 1985.

Wilson, Peter H. *The Holy Roman Empire: A Thousand Years of Europe's History.* London: Allen Lane, 2016.

Winters, Jeffrey A. *Oligarchy.* Cambridge; New York: Cambridge University Press, 2012.

www.ingramcontent.com/pod-product-compliance
Lightning Source LLC
Chambersburg PA
CBHW032115280326
41933CB00009B/849